To the Max

A STORY OF POVERTY, WAR, AND SUCCESS

by
Janis Williams

Front cover: Max in front of BT 13 (Vultee), 1943.

Back Cover: Max piloting the same training plane, Perrin Field, North Texas, January 2, 1944.

FIRST EDITION
Copyright © 2008
Published in the United States of America
By Eakin Press
A Division of Sunbelt Media, Inc.
P.O. Drawer 90159 Austin, Texas 78709-0159
e-mail: sales@eakinpress.com
 website: www.eakinpress.com
ALL RIGHTS RESERVED.
1   2   3   4   5   6   7   8   9
ISBN 978-1-934645-70-3
ISBN 1-934645-70-2
Library of Congress Control Number 2008939927

Cover design by Jennifer Molenaar, sstar78745@yahoo.com
Image editing by Rick Hastie, www.austinwebmedia.com

Contents

Introduction   v

PART ONE: **Growing Up**

1. The Taste of a Copper Penny   3
2. Rooted in the West Virginia Hills   7
3. Life in Akron   9
4. Back to the Backwoods 16
5. Roscoe Avenue 27
6. The Great Depression 35
7. One Boy's Growing Desperation 41
8. A Summer Job 46
9. At Home and on the Streets 47
10. School and the Neighborhood 53
11. Killing Jesse White 60
12. Hard Knocks 62
13. Finding Work 66
14. Restless Wandering 71

PART TWO: **The War**

15. Training 83
16. Austin 93
17. Max Carr, Reporting 98
18. Meanwhile, at Home 104
19. The Ruby Max Didn't Buy 105
20. Chittagong Airport 107
21. Side by Side with Ghurkas 115
22. The C-46 118

23. Days and Nights at War. 122
24. Myitkyina Field 126
25. Dead Reckoning 129
26. Scenes of War. 132
27. Leaving the China-Burma-India Theatre 134

PART THREE: **Home from War**
28. Homecoming. 147
29. Max's New Job. 155
30. Homelife 158
31. Growing Up on Cherry Lane 161
32. The Lake House 166
33. Becoming a Painter. 170
34. Braided Lives. 172
35. Rising in the Phone Company, 1946-1970. 176
36. Providing Presidential Communications. 180
37. A New Face in the Company. 184

PART FOUR: **A New Lease on Life**
38. Cassandra 191
39. Inside an Alaska Prison. 198
40. Searching for Gold 209
41. Doing Business with Ismael. 221
42. Aloft Again. 226
43. Cassandra Rising. 232
44. Travel Snapshots 248
45. Montana. 258

Afterword 263
Appendix: Positive Management Speech. 266

Introduction

My husband, San, and I had been friends with Max and Cassandra Carr for several years when Max had two heart attacks and a stroke. The year was 2006, and he was eighty-five. Up to then he'd been a strong and fit man's man who could fix things, who was a painter, who flew airplanes, pumped iron, traveled widely with Cassandra, and was capable of building a house with his own hands.

One evening while Max was recuperating from these serial health traumas, San and I took soup over to the Carrs, and we stayed to visit awhile. I knew Max was a natural raconteur; I'd heard snatches of his story. For example, I knew he had "flown the hump" in the China-India-Burma theatre during World War II. I knew he'd been highly successful in the phone company, and I'd heard something about a legendary gold mine in Mexico.

But that evening as we talked, it dawned on me that Max's story was both unique and universal. The outline of his life mirrors that of so many in his generation. People who were born in America between 1915 and 1925 were shaped, to a remarkable degree, by two accidents of fate: the Great Depression and World War II. From these historical events, this "Greatest Generation" learned to be frugal, highly responsible, hard-working, and extraordinarily unspoiled.

Today, with health challenges having affected his vision and short-term memory, Max finds himself ready to talk about his life at last. He says, "I've never wanted to delve into it before. For some reason, now I'm willing."

At the encouragement of his highly accomplished wife, Cassandra, Max here examines the charmed life he has lived. In

v

these pages, he reconstructs years of yearning and accomplishment, of adventure, high risk, impulsiveness, and yes, of dreams come to fruition. He examines his journey from poverty to a quiet, hard-earned prosperity.

And he recalls with amazement the fact that he flew 283 combat cargo missions over the Himalaya Mountains, unarmed, facing storms, looming peaks and enemy fire—yet somehow he, unlike many pilots, always returned to safety.

Max Carr's story is emblematic of that generation of young men who, after surviving the Great Depression, reported for service, undertook great risks, and won World War II for the Allies.

The ones who managed to stay alive then dusted themselves off and came home to shape America for a future that, like the mountains beyond the mountains of the Himalayas, they could not begin to see.

Max's life shines as a beacon of hope that adversity can be overcome, and a testament to the power of intelligence, hard work, and ingenuity.

—JANIS WILLIAMS

PART ONE

GROWING UP

1
The Taste of a Copper Penny

"Fear, in case you're wondering, tastes like a copper penny in your mouth. I flew 283 combat missions during World War II, and only once did I taste fear."

In 1944, Max Carr, an ambitious twenty-four-year-old from Akron, Ohio, found himself in the remote regions of India, Burma, and China as a combat cargo pilot in Squadron 14 of the Tenth Combat Cargo Group. He was one of an elite number of World War II pilots who "flew the hump" in the Himalayas, into and out of combat zones, delivering desperately needed supplies to troops fighting on the ground. These young American hotshots maneuvered C-46 airplanes through high mountain passes and directly into the thick of hostilities. To make a delivery was to navigate above rugged terrain and fierce fighting, without any means of defending himself other than via the 45-calibre Thompson submachine gun stored behind each pilot's seat in the cockpit—known as a "grease gun"—and the 45-caliber Colt semiautomatic pistol routinely issued to pilots.

Many of these audacious fly-boys never made it home.

But Max Carr sometimes flew as many as three missions in twenty-four hours, and as he did, he experienced close call after close call. He was shot at, buffeted by gales of wind, and blinded by sun and snow.

Yet the time he experienced that metallic taste in the back of his throat had nothing to do with enemy fire, and for once it wasn't the elements, either.

"I was flying a C-46 on a return trip from the air field in Kunming, China, when we hit a terrific storm. We were winging through the Himalayas to Myitkyina, Burma, where we were based, and as always we were flying specific, pre-determined routes. You've heard of 'Dead Reckoning?'

"The biggest danger while flying in inclement weather was that we had no visual contact outside the cockpit, and we could never know how much the winds were drifting us off course. We didn't know the wind patterns in this uncharted territory. If we were flying in a storm, we'd just make the calculations as best we could.

"Meanwhile, the wind was moving the air mass, and the plane with it. We had no way of knowing whether it was moving us away from, or toward, the mountainside."

Max is in his eighties now, his blue eyes bright and inward-looking as he recalls that night in 1945. "I was piloting a plane that was actually in pretty good shape for the aircraft we were flying at the time.

"We always flew, regardless of the weather, but on this particular night, weather conditions were horrible during take-off. A violent monsoon storm was raging, and shortly after take-off, we were on instrument conditions with zero visibility. I climbed through 10,000 feet, zigzagging among the mountain peaks. At 11,000 feet, I knew I had to start up our superchargers, to improve the carburetion mixture for better combustion. There's a certain way this is done—the mixture control is supposed to be in a low position—and I was always very careful about it.

"However, that day, almost immediately after I started operating my superchargers, the right engine failed and the props started wind-milling. Here we were in a heavy storm, surrounded on all sides by mountain peaks, and the airplane began losing altitude and changing direction, depending on which wind currents we happened to hit."

Even in the best of circumstances, it was difficult to maintain direction and altitude when flying on instruments. That night, though, the peaks that surrounded Max's plane loomed much higher than he was flying, and it was pitch dark outside.

"As soon as I realized we had a problem, I started what we call the single-engine procedure, applying full power to the good engine. The thing to do is get as much power as possible on the good engine, and reduce drag on the failing engine. I went through all the steps, but it was almost impossible to maintain heading and altitude in this violent storm.

"I thought this was it," he says. "We were almost sure to hit one of those peaks. I couldn't tell what the hell was happening. In a quick check of my instruments, I noticed that the cylinder-head temperature read at zero on the engine that was failing. *My God*, I thought. It should be reading at an operating temperature.

"Standing behind me in the cockpit was the crew chief. When I pointed these numbers out, he said the gauge had been malfunctioning. So now, in addition to flying blind, we had little control of the plane. For the moment it was maintaining altitude pretty well, but we didn't know what turbulence was ahead within the storm. And we couldn't see the mountainsides.

"I put out a Mayday call, and yelled for the mechanic to switch on the white lights in the cockpit. I never used these lights because they affect a pilot's night vision, but that night I needed them. The second the lights came on, I noticed the mixture control was in full rich position. That would cause the engine to drown out at that altitude, and fail!"

Max had a new co-pilot on this flight, a cocky kid who had just transferred into the squadron. "I knew immediately what had happened. I had set up the quadrant and all the controls just as I always did. Then, when we put on the superchargers, this idiot co-pilot changed the mixture control, causing that engine to fail.

"Instantly I reached over and pulled the mixture control back into proper position. With that, since I had the throttles completely forward in the maximum operating position, the engine fired back up at full capacity—and flipped the airplane over on its back!

"Keeping my thoughts and emotions in check, I slow-rolled the plane over to normal position. When my pulse finally slowed enough for me to think, I was so furious at that co-pilot I couldn't even look at him. I'd like to have thrown him out of the airplane. I gritted my teeth and said, 'Thanks, buddy. You nearly got us all killed.'

"When we landed, that kid got away from me fast, and I never allowed him to fly with me again. I can't stand that kind of incompetence."

2

Rooted in the West Virginia Hills

Max's parents, Okey Carr and Mary Rollyson, were from deep in the hills of West Virginia. They grew up in adjacent hollows, in an area far from civilization as it was generally understood in the early Twentieth Century, an area where creek beds might serve as roads, and electricity and plumbing were rare.

No one remembers how Okey and Mary met—maybe at one of the meetings or cook-outs that neighbors occasionally had. It can't have been easy for the two young people to meet. They didn't go to church, and families in those West Virginia hills rarely had parties or dances. They kept to themselves, believing that social activities would only distract them from the essential business of survival. Life for hill people was hard, so folks remained focused on eking out a living, most often through coal mining or farming.

Mary, for her part, grew up in Braxton County, a rural area outside the small West Virginia community of Frametown. Her father died when Mary was seven, and from then on, Mary's mother raised the family alone on the family farm. The children included Roy, Amos, Everett, Gertrude (known as Gertie), Mary, Gay, and Matthew (the youngest, who died young). Theirs was a hardscrabble life.

However it happened, Mary Rollyson did meet Okey Carr, and they fell in love. In 1914, a man named Preacher Harvey married them.

The young couple had no illusions that their life together would be easy. They were poor, they had no education, and moreover, there was no work in those West Virginia hills. Poverty was completely ingrained there, and inescapable.

So in 1915, like hundreds or even thousands of others, Mary and Okey said goodbye to family and neighbors and moved to urban Ohio. Life there had to be better, and maybe, they thought, Okey would find work in the rubber tire industry. At the very least, the move would offer an escape from the searing poverty in the West Virginia hills.

Once settled in Akron, the young couple met other families from similar backgrounds. The city had become a magnet to people from the coal mines. Some lived on farms on the outskirts of Akron. Others purchased land, or worked in factories around the city.

3

Life in Akron

Akron was known as "The Rubber Capital of the World," and since Okey Carr was willing to do almost any kind of work, he soon got a job at the Mohawk Tire and Rubber Company. As news of available work reached West Virginia, various relatives began to follow the young couple to the city.

However, not long after starting his job at Mohawk, Okey had a work-place accident, breaking his jaw on one of the machines. Once again he found himself pounding the pavement, looking for work. Once again, it seemed, only hard labor came his way. After a while he was hired on as a fireman on a Baltimore & Ohio Railroad crew, shoveling coal into steam locomotives. This was backbreaking work, but Okey lasted for a while before switching jobs to become a boilermaker for the Akron, Canton & Youngstown Railroad. Now he would be repairing locomotives. Things were looking up.

But his new job, too, proved brutal. When steam engines came in from their runs, they were fire-hot. Okey's job as a boilermaker required that he empty the burning ashes out of the firebox. Then Okey would climb into that firebox and find bad flues, meaning the pipes that the steam ran through. When he found a leak, he would cut out and replace that section of pipe—in the process breathing hot, acidic air. Over time, this destroyed Okey's lungs, a hard consequence of his work, and painful for his family to watch.

The irony of his escaping the black lung of West Virginia's coal mines only to come to the city and develop respiratory problems was too sad to talk about, but it was an irony that everybody in the family understood.

Not long after they arrived in Akron, Okey and Mary started having children. Ford was born in 1916, followed by Juanita the next year. Max came along in November 1919.

A few years later, when it came time to go to kindergarten, Max didn't want to go. School didn't sound fun at all. "Ford and Juanita would walk me to school," he recalls, "and then they would leave for their own class. As soon as they did, I would race home. For three days in a row, I just ran home as soon as I was dropped off. For those three days, Mom didn't take me back to school, though she did scold me.

"Then, on the fourth day, I came walking back toward the house as usual. My Uncle Everett and Mother were sitting on the porch, and Mother told me I was going to get a whipping. I ran away as fast as I could.

"Uncle Everett had a black Model-T Ford, and he and Mom got in that car and started after me as I scurried down the road. I remember cutting across the street at Bittaker Avenue. In a field along the way, I saw a bunch of pipes about four feet in diameter. I ducked into one, but Mother and my uncle had seen me, and they caught up with me. They gave me a licking and marched me back to school.

"After that whipping, I attended kindergarten every day, but I hadn't given in to the system entirely. It was the custom, every morning, for each of us in the class to answer as the teacher, Miss Keller, wrote our name on the board and read it aloud. She was teaching us what our names looked like when written. She would write my name on the board, but I never answered. She'd write 'Edward Carr' and I would just look down at my hands. My name was Max. Nobody ever called me Edward.

"One incident, though, made me realize I actually liked school." Max's eyes twinkle as he goes on, "Miss Keller was very young. Every day right after lunch, we children had to lie down on the floor and take a ten- or fifteen-minute nap. She would walk among us to be sure we were sleeping. On the day in question, I was lying on the floor, fully compliant. Just as I looked up Miss Keller walked by and I saw, to my shock, that she wasn't wearing underwear. I knew I wasn't supposed to be looking, so I shut my eyes tight. Little did I realize that kindergarten was the start to a lifetime of learning!"

Max describes himself as having been rambunctious in grade school. "If I had something to say, I said it, even if the teacher was talking at the time. Finally, in second or third grade, my teacher had had enough of this, and she taped my mouth shut." He chuckles. "I doubt that type of treatment would be tolerated today."

When Max was in first grade, Glenn was born, and Mary Louise came a few years after that. With every additional mouth to feed, Okey found himself working harder, and longer, to provide for his family.

Then, just when it seemed things couldn't get worse, the Great Depression hit. With that, the Carr family's bad luck escalated until, in a final blow, Okey fell ill.

Max recalls, "Everything went wrong at once. I was about ten when Dad got sick, and one thing piled on top of another for him. He was not an educated man, which meant his options were limited. He used to describe himself as a hard-working hillbilly who just wanted to support his family. When I remember Dad from my boyhood, I see a tragic figure."

Yet Okey never stopped trying and, from time to time, good things did happen. After Ford was born, for example, the Carrs managed to buy a lot on Roscoe Avenue in East Akron, a newly developing part of the city. Immediately Okey and his brother-in-law Everett set about building a house for the family.

"You could do that then," Max says. "There weren't the zoning laws and restrictions we have today. Dad had barely managed to afford the lot, and he certainly couldn't afford to hire a contractor or builder. Besides, he figured he knew how to build things as well as any of those fellows. So he and Uncle Everett built our house with their own hands, out of whatever materials they could trade for, buy, or scrounge. The house was sturdy and well-built, but it was tiny for a family our size. I estimate that the foundation was no greater than twenty feet by thirty feet. In fact, it was so small that Dad had to slant the upstairs walls upward in order to accommodate the roof, resulting in side walls no more than three feet high. Ford's and my room, which was more like an enclosed loft or attic, had two windows, and it was just big enough for two beds, side by side, and a dresser. The one dark closet, about two-and-a-half feet deep, used to terrify me when I was a child, because I always imagined something was going to reach out of the blackness and nab me."

Ford and Max slept in one bed, and they argued endlessly. "You're on my side of the bed."

"No, you move over!"

Meanwhile, two windows on one side of the bedroom provided the only ventilation. During blistering summertime nights, the boys' sheets were soaked with sweat by morning.

As the family ballooned, Mary Louise and Juanita slept in the other half of their parents' sleeping nook, and the two brothers, joined eventually by a third, remained upstairs in that same cramped room, with a double bed and a single, fighting every night over whose turn it was to sleep alone.

"When our cousins came to stay with us," Max recalls, "we would alternate heads with feet in the bed, and sleep like sardines."

Downstairs, meanwhile, the family living room was barely big enough to contain a sofa, an armchair, an end-table, a straight chair by the doorway, and a stand-up Philco radio. When the house was built, in 1918, the family had water and gas, but no toilet. They used an outhouse.

"We had a small dining room with a dresser containing dishes, etc., and then a tiny table and chairs," Max says. "The room couldn't have been ten feet by ten feet."

Okey was enterprising, though. He kept adding to the house, doing all the carpentry and building himself, with the help of relatives, chiefly Mary's brother Everett.

When Max was still a pre-schooler, Okey decided the family needed a basement, which would enable him to put in a furnace and also connect to the neighborhood sewer. But how does one build a basement for an already existing house?

"My Dad and Uncle Everett just started digging," explains Max. "Using a team of horses and a three-foot dirt scoop, they began scooping out the land adjacent to the house. I remember watching the process. They excavated a hole about eighteen feet by twenty feet. Then Dad used telephone company conduit tile, which was cheaper than concrete tile, to build the four walls of the basement. As soon as it was completed, they actually moved the house over. It took a team of horses and maybe a truck, but Dad managed to position the house on top of the basement."

Next Okey installed a bathroom, including bathtub, toilet, and a small sink, right next to the stairs. "We had to go through the bathroom to get down to the basement," says Max.

Later still, Okey built a small addition onto the back of the house, and that addition became the kitchen. It was sitting flat on the ground. Max, then about eleven years old, volunteered to dig out a basement underneath the kitchen. The basement room, too, would be small, only about ten by ten, with a small hole in one wall that would eventually become a window. Max tunneled in under the floor, and every day he dug and dug to expand the excavation. "I would pitch the dirt through that hole, and when it had piled up, I'd go outside and spread it around," he says.

This went on for weeks—every day after school, on weekends. Even then, Max was a hard worker. He says, "I damn near dug the foundation out from under that room. Dad had to reinforce the floor."

As he worked, one bald light bulb hung down in the growing hole, shedding just enough light to allow him to keep digging.

"One day, the light bulb shorted out while I was holding it," he says. "Suddenly I was being electrocuted. I started screaming.

"Mother saw what was happening and yelled, 'Drop it!' But I couldn't drop it. My hands were constricting as alternating currents surged through my body. I was standing on damp earth, and I understood I had to act fast. I pulled with all my might, and I broke that electrical cord. If I hadn't managed to do that, I wouldn't be here to tell this story."

14   **To the Max**

MAX'S COUSIN EUGENE BRANNON

Max and I are just about the same age. He's two weeks older than I. His mother, my Aunt Mary, was my mother's sister.

When I was growing up, it was quite an occasion for me to visit the Carrs in Akron. I was accustomed to a rural, backward life in West Virginia, and being able to go to a city was a very big thing for me.

Max's family and mine grew up about 180 miles apart, which was quite a distance in those days. Even so, my family went to Akron when they could, and Max's family came to West Virginia. And when Max and Ford were finally old enough to drive, the two of them would come to see us. We managed to get together quite frequently, in fact, especially after we were teenagers. Max really enjoyed coming to the country because we could do things down here that he couldn't do in the city. At the same time, I enjoyed going to the city. The immensity of the big city, the hustle and bustle. It was all so new to me. Ice cream cones were readily available! What a treat!

The Carrs' house was on Roscoe Avenue, a two-story house, but definitely space was at a premium when we visited. Even so, I remember big, happy visits. For me, visiting Max's

house, with all those siblings and that exciting city life—boy, that was the big time.

Believe me, though, Max's dad was a strict disciplinarian. Uncle Okey. I remember the peach tree switches and it wasn't uncommon for him to use the belt on the boys. To tell the truth, I was scared of him. I didn't want to do anything to cross Uncle Okey. Most of us kids kept a wide berth.

But I respected Uncle Okey because he did his best to provide for his family. He worked for the railroad, but of course he was out of work during the Depression. Even so, I never heard any of the Carrs express a desire to come back to West Virginia. At that time, there was no work in the hills. I remember that so well, all the poverty.

However, my family was fortunate because, in October 1928, my dad quit a job that he'd been on for quite a few years, and went to work for a new company building a plant about a quarter of a mile from where he had been working. For the first several years, he worked seven days a week. He felt lucky just to have a job. When finally the company was in operation, Dad was able to cut back to six days a week. Eventually, he got it down to five-and-a-half days a week, but that took decades. He worked for that company—Union Carbide and Carbon—for thirty-four years.

As a result we, unlike other members of the family, were not impoverished. We managed. We lived near a little place in the northern part of the state called Pine Grove, in Wetzel County, right at the base of the Panhandle near the Pennsylvania border.

Today, the younger generation of the family still lives on the family farm in Braxton County, two and a half miles from Frametown, on the road to Rosedale.

4

Back to the Backwoods

In the summer of 1924, when Max was four years old, his mother took him with her on a trip to visit family in the West Virginia hills. Since Okey worked for the railroad, the family got free railroad passes; otherwise they couldn't have afforded the trip.

In those days, trains were pulled by old steam locomotives. Max remembers waking up as the train pulled through Wheeling, West Virginia. He looked out the train window and saw dozens of blast furnaces going full force. Today he would recognize that he was seeing a steel town, but at the time, eyes wide as saucers, he looked at his mother and asked, "Is the world on fire?"

When they arrived in Frametown, Mary's brother Roy was waiting at the train station with two horses and a buckboard wagon. Uncle Roy drove the horses and Max sat next to him on the wooden seat. They headed deeper and deeper into the hills. When the road ran out, they traveled up creek beds.

The wagon rode rough. Max had on a pair of Little Lord Fauntleroy pants, with a button flap in the back. "Well, the buttons broke," he reports, "and my little ass was showing, which embarrassed me and made me cry. Who wants to visit your relatives with your butt showing?

"We rode for what seemed like hours, until finally we reached the house of the preacher who had married my parents, Preacher Harvey. While we were there, my mother asked for safety pins so she could pin my pants up. I'd probably been worrying her about it. I guess that took care of the problem, because

16

we went on to Uncle Roy's log cabin for several days. That trip was only the first of many the family took to West Virginia," he muses. "I guess you could say those hills were our ancestral home."

Five years later, in December 1929, Okey and Max visited the hills again, and this time they found a road where none had been before. "We were able to go down this isolated road to the log cabin where my mother had been born, and where Uncle Roy still lived. As we drove up in front, I saw kids spilling out of the windows and doors, and slipping away into the woods. They remained hidden the whole time we were there.

"I asked Uncle Roy what the matter was, why his kids had scampered away like that, and he said, 'They're not used to people.' Those cousins stayed isolated until they were drafted into the military during World War II. I've often wondered what military service was like for them. They'd never been part of civilization, never even seen a train. Until they were drafted and went away to war, my cousins knew only the woods and animals and traditions of the West Virginia hills."

Max was nine years old on that rabbit-hunting trip with Okey. "It was twenty below zero, and there were three of us hunting—Dad, a friend of his named Guy Smith, who was a fireman in Akron, and I. Mr. Smith hunted with a beat-up hammer-lock rifle. We drove down the road in a green Model-A Ford, and we saw an old grey horse standing out in this blizzard. Mr. Smith turned to Dad and said, 'Anybody who leaves a horse out in this weather ought to be horse-whipped himself!' That made an impression on me.

"At one point, we had to stop and put chains on the tires to keep the car from sliding into the ditches at the side of the road. Then, just as we were going through the mountains, one of the chains came off a rear wheel and the car rolled down this old country road, and couldn't be turned around, so Dad asked me to go back and get the chain. I did as I was told, but I was so cold I couldn't feel my fingers.

"Eventually we made it down to the ancient log cabin where Uncle Ben lived. He was Dad's older brother. Inside was a fireplace that must have been five feet across, with a fire roaring in its hearth. We thawed out in front of that fire."

Present in addition to Okey, Guy Smith, Max, and Uncle Ben were a couple of elderly relatives. "We sat around that fire long into the night," Max recalls. "Nobody said anything to me about bedtime. The men were drinking whiskey that Uncle Ben had made in the still above his blacksmith shop, and they told stories of the old days there in the mountains. Those stories reached all the way back to the Civil War, which was probably the last time people in these hollows had been disturbed.

"I watched the fire crackling, feeling the heat from it, listening to the stories. The front of my body was warm, but my back, which faced the drafty cabin, was made of ice. At one point, the men started talking about the last mountain lion killed in the area. Uncle Ben described the cat as seven feet from the tip of its nose to the tip of its tail. I could close my eyes and see it. I shuddered. As they held forth, they drank Uncle Ben's moonshine, and spat tobacco juice. I can hear the crackle of tobacco juice hitting the fire, and see myself as a nine-year-old kid trying to get my face closer to the warmth. Even as young as I was, I knew I was lucky to be with men who were such pure examples of a passing way of life.

"But I don't mean to romanticize the mountain people. They were hard. I'll give you an example. Uncle Ben had a daughter, my cousin. She was a beautiful red-head, one of six or seven kids in that family, and about ten years older than I. She had a brother who was two years older still. Now I don't understand this, and as a young kid I understood it even less, but here's what happened: this boy cousin playfully grabbed his sister's breast, and she whirled around with a knife and stuck that knife clear through his hand, jamming it deep into the table. I wasn't a witness to this, but of course it entered the family lore.

"Yep, those mountain people were pretty rowdy.

"In fact, I was always told that my grandmother came from the James family of West Virginia. That was the family of the famous outlaw, Jesse James. The story goes that my grandmother's brother, my Great-Uncle Billy James, was working his farm in the hills one day when two horsemen rode up. He peered at them, and saw they were his cousins, so he invited them to put up and feed their horses and then have supper with him and his wife.

"The next morning, Billy's wife prepared breakfast for their guests, after which the two men saddled up and rode away. Minutes later, when Billy and his wife cleared the breakfast table, they found ten-dollar gold pieces under each of their plates. That was a fortune in those days."

It later emerged that Jesse and Frank James, Billy's cousins, had robbed the 21st Street Bank in Huntington, West Virginia, a day or two earlier. In fact, when they passed through Billy's farm, they'd been on their way back to Missouri, where they lived. Missouri was a great locale for them, because so many trains passed through Kansas and Missouri, and the gang was pulling off dozens of train robberies.

The James brothers were only one of several Old West gangs operating in the years after the Civil War. "Gangs were fairly common back then," Max says, "and the families hidden in the West Virginia hills kept the gangs' stories alive. That was because many hill people had some connection to the outlaws. The Youngers, the James boys."

Outlaws

Like many fed-up ex-Confederates, the James Brothers had learned how to raid and thieve during the Civil War. They, along with Cole Younger of the Younger Brothers, had been with a famously fierce Civil War guerrilla band called Quantrill's Raiders. Between 1854 and 1865, Quantrill and his men conducted guerilla raids in the Confederate cause, though toward the end of that time, both Cole Younger and Frank James left to join the regular Confederate Army.

Max wondered why the miscreants didn't go back to their normal lives after the war. "I asked that question once," he says, "and I was told they weren't allowed to come back home. They were harassed and mistrusted by the police and their neighbors."

Whatever their motivation for stepping back into criminal lives, the James brothers had one exceptional gift: they were unusually good at evading capture. While they were on the loose, historian John N. Edwards wrote of Jesse and Frank James, in his book *Noted Guerrillas*:

Since 1865, it has been pretty much one eternal ambush for these two men—one unbroken and eternal hunt twelve years long. They have been followed, trailed, surrounded, shot at, wounded, ambushed, surprised, watched, betrayed, proscribed, outlawed, driven from State to State, made the objective points of infallible detectives, and they have triumphed. By some intelligent people they are regarded as myths; by others as in league with the devil.

Eventually, of course, Jesse James was killed, and Frank surrendered. Years later, on October 5, 1882, Frank explained his reasons for having surrendered so many years earlier:

I was tired of an outlaw's life. I had been hunted for twenty-one years. I had literally lived in the saddle. I had never known a day of perfect peace. It was one long, anxious, inexorable, eternal vigil. When I slept, it was literally in the midst of an arsenal. If I heard dogs bark more fiercely than usual, or the feet of horses in a greater volume of sound than usual, I stood to arms. Have you any idea of what a man must endure who leads such a life? No, you cannot. No one can unless he lives it for himself.[1]

[1]http://www.civilwarstlouis.com/History/jamesgang.htm

"Frank James once wrote a letter to my Great-Uncle," Max says. "Before he died, Great-Uncle Billy gave the letter to my mother's brother, my Uncle Everett, who carried that letter in his hip pocket from then on. Another connection between our family and the gang is that, to this day, my cousin Jimmy Brannon has a pistol with Jesse James' name engraved under the handle. Not that we admired the outlaws. But they were famous, and they were interesting."

Concludes Max of these distant familial ties, "I warned Cassandra that she was marrying into an outlaw family!"

Max believes the Civil War had a profound effect on West Virginians. Even as remote from society as their lives were, the mountain people couldn't escape the fighting.

"I spent a lot of time with my mother's mother," says Max. "She was born in the 1840s, which would put her in her early twenties during the Civil War. She often talked about how many families had brothers fighting on opposite sides—one for the south, the other for the north. Yet she said that when everyone came home for a reunion or holiday, the War Between the States wasn't even mentioned. It was forgotten.

"West Virginia had the same problem Missouri did, in that the state was divided, which meant that families were divided. But when hillbilly soldiers came home, they left their differences on the battlefield."

Max says his Grandmother Rollyson could have been the model for the painting *Whistler's Mother*. "She was a tiny woman who wore her white hair in a knot at the nape of her neck. She was prim, domestic, a person who had grown up in the 1800s on hard land. I can still see her sitting in a rocking chair, probably wearing a gingham housedress. She wore glasses on the end of her nose, and I always thought she looked exactly the way a grandmother should look.

"Grandmother used to tell me about her childhood, living off the land, the family growing its own food, raising everything they needed to survive.

"One day I commented to Grandmother Rollyson that I didn't understand her love of the land. This shocked her. How could anybody not love the land? I've always regretted that careless remark, because I'm sure she thought less of me for it.

"The notable thing about Grandmother was that she seemed content with her life," says Max. "She outlived two husbands, she had a good family, and she even owned a little property. None of that had been guaranteed to previous generations of her family as they set out from Cork County, Ireland, penniless, heading to America."

Whenever they visited West Virginia, the Carrs stayed at

Grandmother Rollyson's wide-faced house, with its big wooden porch running across the front. It was made of rough-hewn lumber, unpainted. Grandmother's second husband was an old man who liked to sit rocking on that porch and contemplate the stream running vigorously a few feet away. "He had a waist-length white beard, and he always wore overalls," Max says. "I'm sure he was bone-tired by the time I knew him. He'd been a farmer, after all, and spent his life eking a living out of that dirt. He must have been in his eighties when I knew him, and life expectancy wasn't what it is now.

"Once when I was only four or five years old, I was wading in the stream when suddenly I tripped on a stone and fell in, slipping quickly under the water's surface. Ford, meanwhile, was playing on the bank. I heard Grandpa holler, 'Ford! Grab his hand!' and with that I knew enough to extend my own hand. Ford pulled me out of the water."

Max spent several boyhood summers working in West Virginia. "The hills were steep and people raised their own corn and foodstuffs. The hills were dotted with log cabins and rough lumber houses, and families had outhouses for toilets. Living was basic, with meals made up entirely of whatever people could raise. Cornbread and buttermilk were mainstays. For breakfast, there were biscuits hot out of that old wood-burning cook stove, always served with bacon or sausage that had been butchered the previous winter. Much of the food was pickled and stored in big wooden crocks, or in quart fruit jars—peppers, pickled beans, corn. I especially remember the pickled green beans.

"As to the meat, it was stored in dugouts where the temperature stayed cooler. This kept the meat edible, but eventually it would develop a mold in that dampness. When it did, our relatives would just cut the mold off and fry the meat. I assume there wasn't anything poisonous in it, because we all ate it, and nobody died. Seasoning? Morton's salt. Period.

"When I was old enough, I took part in the hog-killing. Normally, if my grandfather had a gun, he would shoot the hog. I can just picture the scene. First they would shoot the hog, then stick the whole carcass down in a big tub of boiling water to clean it off, and finally hang it on the tripod. Then the men would butcher it. We cured the meat with salt. Here's my only other memory of my Grandpa: the hog had been shot, and as Grandpa was butchering the meat, he put the bloody knife in his mouth when he needed to free his hands. I was appalled by this. What a primitive gesture. Who would put a bloody knife in his mouth? Even though I was just a little boy, I was shocked when I saw that. I reminded myself he wasn't my real grandfather. He just married my grandmother after my real grandfather died in Montana.

"Uncle Everett worked in a slaughterhouse, where they used a sledgehammer to kill the animals. They would just hit the animal in the head. I guess they didn't have the money to spend on ammunition."

Okey's brother Ben was an entrepreneurial sort. He owned a blacksmith shop, but that was not all. "In addition to the blacksmith shop, he had a rural . . . well, I won't say it was a store," Max says, "because most people today wouldn't even call it that. It had shelves, and I guess there must have been some merchandise on exhibit, but what I remember most is Mail Pouch tobacco, because my dad used to chew it. In any case, Uncle Ben's was the only place resembling a store in the vicinity.

"Bolted to the shelf-lined wall was a primitive building made of vertical siding and some logs. Uncle Ben used that as a shed, and next to *that*, in ramshackle fashion, was a great big millstone. Powering it from the creek, Uncle Ben would grind corn for all the people in the area. Everybody raised corn.

"Next to the millstone was his blacksmith shop—and above that, his still. The still was no doubt illegal, but the people there were so deep in the hills and so isolated that they had the perfect setting for making homemade corn liquor. However, Uncle Ben didn't make his moonshine to sell; it was strictly for his own and his friends' consumption. I never saw them actually make moonshine, because I was too young to know what was going on, but I did see the facilities a few times."

To Max, the people in the hills were peaceful, with each family forming its own universe. Their orbits were extremely narrow, and interaction among families was minimal. "I don't remember problems with theft, or violence," Max says, "but we all knew about those few feuding families. Of course, the Hatfields and the McCoys, near the Kentucky-West Virginia border, were famous for their feud.

"Actually, when he was a young man, my dad had lived with Devil Anse Hatfield. Dad was working as a lumberjack on the border of West Virginia and Kentucky at the time, and he took a room at Devil Anse Hatfield's house.

"The Hatfield and McCoy feud started over the theft of a hog, and it just grew from there." Max chuckles. "Contrary to Grandmother Rollyson's claim, not all mountain families left the Civil War on the battlefield."

According to Max, his dad had several photos of Devil Anse sitting on his porch in a rocking chair in front of a typical hillside house. "The photo was framed in our house when we were growing up," Max reports. "Dad seemed to think the Hatfields and McCoys were just typical backwoods families who had a little misunderstanding, and settled it the way hill people settle matters."

The Hatfields and the McCoys

The famous Hatfield vs. McCoy feud, which came to symbolize feuding families everywhere, took place in the mountain terrain of Eastern Kentucky and West Virginia. The McCoys lived on the Kentucky side of the Tug River, and the Hatfields on the West Virginia side. Initially, the two families crossed the river back and forth in friendship. There were even some marriages between the clans, who remained cordial until the Civil War.

Both families were Southern sympathizers, but one of the McCoys, a young man named Harmon, decided to serve for a year in the Union Army. He broke his leg while he was a soldier, and he was discharged on December 24, 1864. When he returned home, he was warned by one of the McCoy clan, an uncle named Jim Vance, that the Logan Wildcats—Confederate marauders headed by Devil Anse—would be calling on him. Soon thereafter, Harmon was at his well drawing water when he heard gunshots.

Harmon's slave, Pete, had hidden food and water in a nearby cave, in case Harmon had to hide from his enemies. On hearing gunshots that day, Harmon made for his hiding place. However, the Wildcats tracked Pete's footprints in the snow and apprehended Harmon as he hid in the cave. They shot him to death on January 8, 1865.

Everyone in the holler, including Harmon's family, had considered Harmon's military service disloyal, so people agreed that he had brought his murder on himself. No one was ever charged or tried for it.

For a time after that, things remained calm between the two families. Then, in the autumn of 1878, the patriarch of the McCoy family, Old Randall (who was, in fact, married to a Hatfield), thought he spotted one of his pigs being stolen by his wife's Hatfield relative, Floyd. Infuriated, Old Randall demanded that Floyd be brought to trial.

The trial did take place, and the final verdict hinged on the testimony of Old Randall's nephew, Bill Staton, who said the pig in question had actually belonged to Floyd Hatfield. To further complicate matters, the jury for Floyd's trial was made up of six Hatfields and six McCoys. The deadlock was broken when one of the McCoy jurors sided with the Hatfields. Old Randall lost the case, and Floyd Hatfield was acquitted.

Within weeks, Bill Staton was shot to death by Paris and Sam McCoy, who wound up pleading self-defense and were acquitted.

Meanwhile Randall had a pretty daughter named Roseanna, who fell in love with Devil Anse's son, Johnse Hatfield. One night, Roseanna slipped off with Johnse and went to live at Devil Anse's house. Johnse refused to marry her, though, and eventually, at her mother's behest, she came home. But life at home was intolerable now, because it was generally agreed that she had betrayed the family.

Roseanna ran away again and rekindled her love affair with Johnse. One night they were lying in each other's arms when Roseanna's brothers burst in and took Johnse prisoner.

Roseanna borrowed a neighbor's horse and rode bareback, without hat or coat, to tell Devil Anse what had happened. Anse rallied his sons and neighbors and rescued his son without incident. Once again, the lovers were torn apart, but Roseanna soon learned she was pregnant. She returned home, where she contracted measles and lost her baby.

In August 1882, three of the McCoy boys, apparently without provocation, attacked Devil Anse's younger brother, Ellison Hatfield. They stabbed Ellison multiple times and then shot him in the back. Ellison lived for three days, but then he died, at which point the Hatfields dragged the three McCoy brothers across the Tug River, tied them to paw-paw bushes and shot them to death.

Next, the Hatfields broke into the home of Mary McCoy Daniels and whipped her and her daughter with a cow's tail, because they thought she was leaking information to the McCoys. When her brother tried to avenge the whippings, he was promptly shot to death.

On and on it went, for years. The violence included raids, counter raids, the burning down of the McCoy's cabin, the beating deaths of several family members, insanity, suits, counter-suits. Old Randall's daughter, Adelaide, was rumored to have gone mad over the violence. Before the feud was finally over, thirteen people in the two families had died.

5

Roscoe Avenue

The Carrs' house in Akron was on the outskirts of town, and every year the family would rent three or four acres adjacent to their land, cultivate that land, and raise garden crops: corn, beans, beets, potatoes. Nobody had money in those years, so people grew what they could. Even in the city, every family that could eke out the space had a garden.

During Max's early childhood, the family had no electricity so they used oil lamps.

Max and Ford were shaped by this urban neighborhood where the family found itself. Times were hard for nearly everyone as the Depression deepened, but the brothers quickly learned who were the "haves" and who the "have-nots"—and they knew they were in the latter category. This knowledge had a profound effect on them.

Max was always observant, and as a child he turned those powers of observation onto the search for how to escape the poverty that plagued his family. What made for a successful life? he wondered. How did one accomplish it? It was a mystery to him, but one he was determined to solve. To this end, he studied the adults in the neighborhood, including his father.

"I watched my Dad walking the streets almost every day, just looking for some way to feed his family for one more day. It made me sad for him, but it also made me more determined to work hard, and one day to find security in the workplace."

One of the "haves" was Ira Boggs, a bachelor who lived across the street from the family. He, too, was from West Virginia, and Mary Carr always claimed Ira was a distant relation, because there were some Boggses on Okey's side of the family. True or not, Max was aware that Mr. Boggs had the nicest house on the block, that his lawn was always manicured, that he dressed well, and that he always drove new, well-maintained cars.

Even more importantly, Mr. Ira Boggs always had a job. "To me, that made him wealthy as a king," Max recalls. "That made him one of the fortunate few. He *always* had a job and a person with a job was like royalty to me. Even as a young child, I understood how important work would be in my life."

When Max was five or six years old, Mr. Boggs married a beautiful young woman named Annabelle. After only a short time, though, the lady's parents, who lived about a mile away in an apartment building, somehow persuaded Annabelle to leave Mr. Boggs and come home. Throughout Max's childhood, he wondered at this. How sad that these parents wanted their daughter to leave someone as nice as Ira Boggs! Ira was handsome, he lived an orderly life, he was a good person—and he had a job. What more could anybody want?

The Emerson brothers, who lived down the street, also had steady jobs during the Depression. They, along with a few other men from the neighborhood, worked for the telephone company as linemen. Max says, "I came to understand that work could lead to a productive life. Work equaled success." Thus were planted the seeds of his later determination to work harder and longer than anybody.

Years later, after Max started working for the telephone company in Akron, the Emerson brothers were still working for the construction department out on the pole lines. "In fact," Max says, "they worked out on those trucks until the day they retired. At some point I realized that I was three or four levels higher in the company than the Emerson brothers had ever been, in long years working for the company. While I'd progressed into management, they'd been content to stay on the pole lines."

"In the Roscoe Avenue neighborhood, we fit right in," Max recalls. "Dad was pretty handsome in his younger years, and he and Mom both had a lot of friends. People would congregate at our house because my parents were fun to be around, at least until Dad got sick. Some of our guests weren't working class, either, but a strata above. When we were growing up, it was nothing to have fifteen or twenty people at our house, drinking, playing cards, and visiting. Relatives, but also friends. Mom always had big bottles of homemade pickled peppers, which tasted great with one of Dad's quarts of home brew—especially when you were hungry.

"As the Depression wore on, Dad continued to lose heart. Add to that his illness, and the last fifteen or twenty years of his life were pure hell.

"Maybe that's why he was so strict with us. Was Dad fun with the kids? Did he ever joke around? Well, I'd just say that words of praise from him were rare gems. He was more intent on keeping us in line than in showing confidence in us. I honestly did get a whipping almost every day.

"Mom, by contrast, was a rock. Everybody liked her disposition. She was a common sense person, with a high degree of intelligence. We kids felt close to her, partly because she would stand up for us with Dad. One day, for example, I had done something or other wrong, and Mom said, 'When Dad gets home, you're going to get a whipping.' Well, I had this big woolly toboggan, and I asked Mom if she'd tell on me if I stuffed it down my pants so the whipping wouldn't hurt so much. She laughed and promised she wouldn't tell on me.

"Well, sure enough, Dad got home, and he took me down to the cellar, our usual venue for punishment. When he started whipping me, I accidentally laughed, and Dad discovered that toboggan. He took it out and I got a whipping for sure. He liked to use a branch of our peach tree."

Max's older brother Ford tells a similar story. "When Dad got angry with us, Mother would defend us—unless she thought we had it coming," Ford remembers. "One time he was going to get onto me for one reason or another. He started to haul me down to the basement. Dad had a big ol' leather razor strap, and he told me, 'Get in the basement.' But Mother said, 'Don't do it, Okey.'

"'I'm going to knock some sense into him,' Dad muttered.

"But Mother came down the stairs after him, and by the time we got to the bottom of the stairs, Mother was standing a few feet away. She said quietly, 'I'm telling you, Okey. You're wrong. Don't hit him.' She was holding a big old butcher knife, and Dad said, 'What's that for?'

"'If you're going to beat him, I'll cut you,' she said, all menacing. So Dad turned, walked back up the stairs, and put the razor strap away. He just laughed about it." Ford laughs now, remembering the story.

Eugene Brannon, Max's cousin, adds, "Aunt Mary was not as strict as Uncle Okey. She could control her temper pretty well. She was a disciplinarian, but not like my uncle. I always had the impression that Mary was somewhat protective of the kids. If she thought Okey was being unfair, she would stop him. In other words, she was the all-powerful one in the family. She seemed to have the final say. She was a good woman and she was a good mother."

As Okey's health worsened, Max never stopped trying to please his dad. Though Okey and Mary exercised tight control over their five kids, and definitely taught the children right from wrong, their energies remained sapped by trying to put food on the table. They were focused on surviving.

Max began to yearn for escape, not so much from his family as from the despair he saw all around him. Now and then he would find something to fix that yearning on, and he would dream and dream of this new desire.

"Growing up, I wanted nothing so much as a bike," he says.

"I could close my eyes and imagine riding down the street on my very own bike. I could imagine the envy the other poor kids would feel. But I had no way of getting a bike. It was impossible. I would have done anything, I would have worked until I dropped, but it was completely beyond my grasp."

Ford Carr, Max's older brother

No question about it, there were hard times when we were growing up. We boys appreciated everything that was given to us, and the help that was extended. It was always good to be invited into some of the homes where the people were a little more fortunate, especially if we were hungry. We had a neighbor across the street, for example, who used to let me wash his car. It was a big deal to make fifty cents. He was a bachelor, and at times he'd take us out to eat. That was big time—because we couldn't afford to go out. Ira Boggs was his name.

We had good neighbors. There were three brothers who lived on the street, each with his own house. The Emerson boys, we called them. They all worked for the phone company, and they were good to us. I was impressed that all three were very good ball players. They played for the Akron Police Department ball team. I was batboy for them, and I'd get to go with them to games. It was some-

thing else to get to ride a bus. At twelve or thirteen years of age, during a period of economic Depression, these things really impress a kid.

Dad was hard-nosed. Everything had to be just right, or he'd knock our heads off. If he had a club, he'd use that, too. I can't count the times I made him mad. Very young in life, probably in his forties, he had a terrible illness that handicapped him some, but if he could walk he'd work. He always managed to find some kind of work somewhere. He'd put groceries on the table. For a long time, he worked as a boilermaker for the railroad. Meanwhile, Mother had five of us, and that was enough for her. Providing for a big family was hard on Dad, I know it was.

He was only seventy-two when he died. In the end, I think he just gave up. He was a heavy smoker, yes, and he had emphysema. But I'm telling you, it was the Great Depression that did him in.

Yearning was endemic in the neighborhood, and not just among the children. Sometimes neighbors met with disaster as they scrambled to save pennies. When he was a child, Max observed one such incident at close range, and the memory of it still burns.

It happened one afternoon when Max was in grade school. He and Ford were bored and looking for something to do on that sunny Saturday afternoon in 1928. The sky was clear and blue as the brothers moseyed the quarter of a mile or so to the clay pit, an area near the house on Roscoe Avenue, where clay soil was excavated for making pottery. After years of digging into that terrain, workers had created a cavern about a quarter of a mile wide and a hundred feet deep, and this had become a favorite play spot for neighborhood children who liked to climb on the clay banks and jump off, or chase each other, or play hide and seek.

When Max and Ford arrived that day, as was usually the case, others from the neighborhood were milling around the pit—a few kids, and also other people the Carr boys knew, including the boys' neighbors, Mr. Post, Mr. Wise, Mr. Shemko, and two of Mr. Post's sons, older teenagers.

Over time, a vein of coal had been unearthed on one side of the excavated pit. This vein was too small for a mining company to bother with, but it was coal nonetheless. People in the city were poor, and they were cold. This was the Depression, after all, and these men needed to find a way to heat their homes.

As they approached the clay pit's eighty- to ninety-foot walls, Max and Ford noticed the men trying to dig the coal out, throwing dirt behind them as they dug. That dirt was piling up on the slope ten to fifteen feet below. What fun to jump into those soft piles, Max and Ford thought as they climbed midway up the sheer cliff.

As he was climbing up the ledge for a second go, Max overheard Mr. Post say, "We should reinforce this." Max saw that the only thing holding up that overhang were three picks standing metal side up and wedged in under the roof of the excavation.

One of the other men answered, "Oh, hell, it won't fall in."

Max jumped—and at the same moment the whole cliff collapsed. It wasn't properly shored up, of course. When the ledge gave way, Ford was knocked off and partially buried.

Ford takes up the story. "Laurence Post was with me, and in an instant I was covered with dirt, with only my right arm and my head above the ground. Somebody dug me out, laid me over to the side and said, 'We've got to get these other fellows out.'"

Looking around them, the boys realized that Mr. Post, Mr. Wise, and Mr. Shemko, along with the Post brothers, had all been buried under tons of loose dirt. "I was horrified to see Edwin Post's leg sticking up out of the dirt," Max says. "The image of his leg and foot, wearing a brogan shoe, is burned into my memory. I turned away, dizzy, and when I returned my gaze to that spot in the pile of dirt seconds later, that foot was gone, buried with the rest of Edwin's body. He was only about sixteen years old, and in an instant he was dead."

Max and Ford backed away in shock.

"We have to get help!" Max cried.

But Ford's leg was badly injured, and he could barely walk. He leaned on Max's shoulder as the two boys limped away, both sobbing. To get out of there, they had to climb up the shifting walls of clay, and when they got to the top and staggered down the street, they spotted two young men sitting on the front porch of a nearby house.

"What's wrong?" the young men asked as the boys approached, and Max managed to choke out a stammered report of the cave-in. "All those people are buried!" he cried. "All of them are completely buried. I think they're dead."

"Are you sure?" asked the young men, wide-eyed, and Max assured them that he'd seen the avalanche with his own eyes.

There were no telephones in the area, but there were red boxes on telephone poles whose purpose was to signal the fire department. Max and Ford had always been coached never to play with the red boxes; they were only for emergencies.

Well, this was an emergency!

In a flash, one of the young men broke open the box and pulled the lever. Meanwhile, the other young fellow piled the Carr brothers into his black Model-T and took them home, two little boys in shock, completely traumatized.

Ford had to get to the doctor, and meantime the fire department arrived on the scene. The boys' uncle was in the fire department, and he later reported having seen the bodies. As feared, everyone was dead.

"If I hadn't jumped just when I did," Max recalls today, shaking his head, "I would have been covered up, too."

When Max thinks of the Post family, he wonders how Mrs. Post managed after losing her husband and two of her sons. "What must have happened to the mother, and to the remaining family? There were no social services in those days, and women couldn't really work. The family must have gone on welfare, which at that time consisted of getting chits for buying food. That's all there was for poor widows during the Depression. It was such a tragedy."

"That's true," agrees Ford, now in his nineties. "We learned a lot from growing up the way we did. What we learned was how to handle trouble."

As for Max, it turned out this was only one of many near-death experiences he would undergo in his life. "Yes." He nods in wry agreement. "I suppose I've had plenty of close calls."

6

The Great Depression

The Roscoe Avenue neighborhood had been new when the Carr family first arrived, but by the time Max and Ford were in junior high, it had grown and attracted a variety of immigrants: Russians, Czechs, Slavs, Poles, and blacks made up the neighborhood. New families were building homes behind Roscoe, on Ardella Street. The Depression was wearing on the neighbors, and hope was in short supply as the Carr boys approached their teens. The expanding ethnic make-up of the neighborhood soon allowed territorialism to set in. Street gangs began to form.

Max started getting in trouble. "One time early on—I had to be less than ten years old—I set the dump on fire. I really was a young arsonist. This particular incident took place during the day, and before I knew it, the fire engines were all on the scene. When my mother found out what I had done, she told me I was going to jail. I took her literally, and I went in and took a bath in the wash tub. I got dressed in my Sunday best and combed my hair. I was accepting my fate. I was getting ready to go to jail.

"When nobody came for me, I was so relieved. I swore I'd never mis-step again."

However, this was a promise Max could not keep. Even as pre-teens, he and Ford had to be hoodlums if they were going to survive on the streets. "One kid lived a block or two over," Max recalls. "A very deprived kid, but he had one of the most beautiful singing voices I'd ever heard. When side shows visited our end of town, this kid would sing "That Wild, Irish Rose," and the crowd would go crazy.

"Well, he had a .22 rifle. In fact, a lot of the young kids in our neighborhood had guns. Because he had such a sweet voice, I assumed he was a good kid. But when he was around ten years old, and I was twelve, this boy with the angel voice shot my friend Walter Mlynar in the stomach, just to see how Walter would react.

"I remember a neighbor named Mr. Lucas grabbed Walter up and rushed him to the hospital. While they were on the way there, a traffic policeman stopped the two of them and warned Mr. Lucas not to speed—but he sure didn't offer to escort him to the hospital.

"As far as I know, nothing ever happened to the ten-year-old who did the shooting. Sure, he was very underprivileged, but then we all were. We kids were all poor and hungry, and frustrated as hell. But we didn't go around shooting people. He was just a mean kid."

In fact, the neighborhood was full of punks, all itching for a fight. Once, for example, a couple of boys in the neighborhood came to odds over the sale of a baseball. Max says, "Steve Hudnick was a Russian immigrant kid, nine years old, who owned a baseball that had the whole cover on it, a rarity in our neighborhood. The other boy was sixteen. He was a colored boy, as African-Americans were referred to then, whose name was A.C. Brown. He lived behind us. We called him Cecil. Well, Cecil offered Steve Hudnick a quarter for his baseball, and Hudnick told him he wanted thirty-five cents. Cecil responded that the baseball wasn't worth it.

"This infuriated Hudnick, who went home to get the .22 rifle that his dad had bought him. He then came back and shot Cecil in the stomach.

"Now, Cecil's parents didn't believe in doctors. Their religion held that God would heal Cecil.

"Cecil and I were the same age, so I visited him the day after he was shot. Poor guy was sitting in his front room with just his pants on. A noticeable bullet wound began about waist-high on his back, and then traveled around until I could see the purple bullet underneath his skin. I remember how solemn he looked. I imagine he thought he was going to die.

"Somehow the authorities found out about this and they took him to the hospital, where he recovered. But nothing ever happened to Steve. He was never punished. It must have been considered a minor crime to shoot a colored boy who you think insulted you."

As these events suggest, racism was everywhere in 1930s urban America. Life was hard for black people in the south, but in some ways it was even harder in the industrial north. For Max, the racial climate was played out in tabloid every day, right in his neighborhood. He gives another example. "There was a young man who lived a few streets over. His name was Jasper Johnson, and he was completely inoffensive, but he had one problem: he was colored.

"Jasper worked in a fruit market about a mile from where we lived. Every night about 10:30, when the fruit market shut down, Jasper would come down the street on his way home.

"Well, one night a kid named Johnny Shemko put a sheet over his head, and when Jasper come down this dark road, Johnny jumped out and yelled, scaring Jasper to death. He was a timid fellow, anyway, and he nearly fainted with fear. This incident gave rise to what we called the 'Phantom.' After that, there was always somebody wearing a white sheet and haunting the clay pit.

"Word got around that there was a phantom in the vicinity. Of course, Johnny Shemko was the one who started it all, and his little game went on for a few months. Thanks to me, though, it all came to an end one night when I got spooked.

"It was very late and very dark. I had gone down to the clay pit to shoot my .22. I attached a flashlight to the barrel of the rifle so I could shoot at the rats in the cliff of refuse at the city dump. As usual, Johnny was running around the pit with a sheet over his head. I saw motion, but I couldn't tell who it was. I called out, but Johnny didn't answer, so I tried to shoot him with my rifle. Johnny later told me he had heard bullets whistling by his head that night, and thereafter, he wasn't so interested in the game of Phantom."

Max and his friends always had ready access to firearms. "The guys in this group would get .22 rifles and cut the barrels off, and cut the stock off, and they'd make what they called handguns. It's a wonder more of us weren't shot.'

Max remembers the neighborhood clay pit as the center of his friends' social life. He recalls, "When I was a little kid, the company used a small locomotive called a donkey engine to transport the clay to the factory where potters shaped it into plates, planters, mugs and bowls. Sometimes our dad would get temporary work at the clay pit, testing the donkey engine out after doing some boiler work on it. I would go up to visit him when he was working, and now and then he'd let me ride in the locomotive. He showed me what the driver had to do to operate the throttle, and he even let me operate it a few times.

"I bragged about this to my friends, but they didn't believe me. So one night, right after the little donkey engine had been put away for the night, we opened the door to the shed where it was kept. Steam was still rising from the engine. I fired the locomotive up, backed it out, and ran it down the tracks to the Baltimore & Ohio railroad. Right about then, the steam gave out, and I didn't know what to do about that—so we left that little engine right where it was, on the tracks a mile or two away. That was theft, I now realize. At the time, I only knew I wanted my friends to see I could drive the thing."

In this environment, Max and Ford grew aggressive and they frequently found themselves in fights. They were always ready. "I fought almost every day," Max admits. "Once, I was in a fight with Bobby Mann, a neighborhood kid about my age and size. I don't remember what the fight was about. It didn't much matter. All of us kids were hungry, and we were frustrated. We didn't see much of a future ahead, and fighting was about the only way we had of venting.

"Well, that day Bobby was getting the best of me. I remember I was on the ground and he was sitting on my chest. It wasn't looking good for me.

"Suddenly I looked down the road and saw my dad coming, and I had the thought, I can't let Dad see me get beat. I felt a surge of adrenaline, and sure enough, by the time Dad drew even with us, I had Bobby on the ground and I was sitting on *his* chest."

Another time Ford and Max were running on Arlington Street, just horsing around, and they tripped each other. Arlington was a brick road, and when they fell they were both knocked silly. They looked pretty beaten up, and a couple of guys from outside the neighborhood approached, thinking the brothers had been hit by a car. They offered to help.

Ford said, "Get lost, will ya?"

But the strangers were determined to be of service.

That's when the brothers resorted to the ways of the street. "We beat 'em up," Ford says now. "And they were just trying to be good Samaritans!"

"When Cecil Brown and his family moved into the street behind us, we had our first exposure to black people," says Max. "We all got along. It wasn't race but territory that defined relationships for us kids. If a kid was from our neighborhood, we accepted him. We just didn't like people from other neighborhoods to bother us. Neighborhoods were very clearly defined, too. Nobody could be mistaken about where he belonged."

Ford adds, "One night a couple of boys from another neighborhood were walking down our street. We said, 'Where you guys think you're going?'

"'We're going home,' they said, and tried to push past us.

"But Max and I said, 'You're not going down our street.' A fight erupted. We had determined we had to beat them. It was a matter of pride."

"The area was becoming a tough part of town," Max says.

The clay pit had a cave in its side, and this cave became the neighborhood boys' gang hideout. One day George Grebanya, a neighborhood kid a little older than Max, decided to rob a store. The store owner apparently lived above the establishment, and when Grebanya ran, the owner shot him with buckshot and then called the police to report the robbery. Meanwhile, George ran away and hid out in the gang's cave.

Max takes up the story. "The day after the robbery, some of us went to the hide-out, and we saw he had spent the night there. George's back was just peppered with buckshot. In the end, he had to go to the hospital for treatment. I don't know what the police did to him, but clearly he got caught."

While strenuously defending against outsiders' coming into their neighborhood, Max and Ford and their gang made regular forays into adjacent neighborhoods. Max says, "Our gang would invade the territory of gangs in areas close to ours. Almost everybody had a gang hideout, and we would invade their territory and take, for example, all their *Wild West* magazines. And maybe as we were leaving their hang-out, they would appear, and we'd have a big rumble.

"Gangs were different there. We were just a group of friends. Our group was mischievous, and we got into fights, but we never really harmed anybody," Max concludes.

7

One Boy's Growing Desperation

By the time Max was a teenager, he and his Dad had a close relationship, at least in certain ways. Okey always seemed proud of Max, because the boy had spirit and he was rowdy. Yet even though Max and his dad got along, and even though Max felt deep empathy for his father, Okey never showed the boy affection. Max says, "Never in my life do I remember Dad hugging me, or holding me close. He was not at all affectionate but sometimes, with words, he showed me he cared. Occasionally he would offer a little encouragement. I treasured that.

"On a day-to-day basis, though, he was always working, or looking for work, while Mother struggled to feed us, and clothe us, and keep the house. My parents were both overwhelmed with trying to keep the family afloat, so we kids were left on our own to grow up."

The Carr children went to public schools. "I assume we had good genes, especially from Mother's side of the family," Max says. "She was a good student, and most of us kids were, too."

Ford adds, "Max did all right in school. As a matter of fact, he did well. He was always smart. I remember he was president of the National Honor Society. Actually, even as busy and stressed as our parents were when we were growing up, they always kept after us about grades, especially Mother did. If

41

we ended up with bad grades, we certainly heard about it from her."

Max adds, "I never studied at home, though. My parents used to fuss at me about that. Ford and Juanita were also good students, but they would study at night. However, my memory allowed me to make good grades without much effort. I found it easy to commit information to memory. Teachers and my classmates used to marvel at this. At some point I realized I could read something once and remember it. I've heard this called photographic memory. It was a long time before I comprehended that not everybody could do this.

"It was awe-inspiring to my friends when I gave a book report in eighth grade. I took up the whole class period, because I was able to quote the entire book, except for one paragraph. The teacher didn't stop me, because she couldn't believe what she was hearing. She followed along in the book, and at the end of class, she said I had left out only one paragraph.

"It's interesting to realize that, although my parents were not educated beyond eighth grade, they insisted that we study— even though they had no possible way to send us to college. I think their highest aspiration for us was that we graduate from high school. They probably pictured us in the work force, somewhere in an industry. I'm sure they just hoped we would become basic working people, and be able to find and keep a job. So it's surprising how our lives have evolved."

Max leans forward as he explains. "Ford didn't go to college, but he wound up running a trucking company. He progressed from being a truck driver to becoming head of the company. He started driving tractors and trailers when he was fourteen years old. They used to drive old Diamond-T trucks. This was a premier truck back in the 1930s, an enormous vehicle. And my brother Ford was just a natural in the trucking industry, one of those people who could take a big truck and a trailer and back it up like it was a toy wagon. I could never do that.

"In fact, I remember the first and probably only time I drove a Diamond-T truck, I threw on the air brakes and almost went through the windshield. I just wasn't cut out to be a truck-driver." He chuckles.

Adding to the general mood of deprivation and disheartenment during the Depression was the fact of Prohibition. "It might have been illegal, but Dad always had beer or wine brewing in the basement," Max says now. "The Russian kids in the neighborhood, too, their dads always had wine and beer going. During the Depression, people didn't have money to buy spirits even if spirits had been available, so people made their own. All the immigrant families did.

"I think we were the only family who made beer as well as wine. But we also had more company than anybody else. Our house was open to neighborhood kids and their houses were open to us as well. We kids would drift from house to house, and we were always welcome."

He goes on, "Dad gave me a pretty good education in wine-making. I remember just before I enlisted into the military, I made my own fifty-gallon keg of wine. The recipe included multiple gallons of apple cider and grape juice, mixed with pounds of sugar and raisins. All this I put into a fifty-gallon wooden barrel.

"My parents had taught me to place a rubber tube into a glass of water sitting on top of the keg. The tube was completely sealed in the top so that, as the wine fermented, it would expel gaseous bubbles into this glass of water. I had to keep the glass full of water all the time so that air wouldn't get back into the keg.

"After some weeks, the bubbles stopped appearing in the water, which meant that the fermentation of the grape juice was stopped, and the wine was ready to drink. One night I decided to try it out with Jimmy Grafhorst, a neighborhood boy about my age. I gave Jimmy a glass of that wine just before we kids were going to play poker. Now, Jimmy was an experienced drinker, but after one glass of my wine, he could hardly walk."

Max grins. "Do I have to tell you who won that poker game?

"But there's more to the story of that keg of wine. By that time, my older sister Juanita had married a boy named Lonnie Boyce. Lonnie was four or five years older than I, and an experienced beer drinker. I introduced Lonnie to this wine, and by the time I left for the air force shortly after, Lonnie had drunk forty-eight out of the fifty gallons of my wine. I never drank it myself. I wasn't much of a drinker. I only had one glass, to see if it was any good. I was curious whether I could make a good barrel of wine."

Max was often hungry. In fact, the whole family was hungry. "It was a custom in those days for those who had a farm, when they had a chore like butchering or gathering a crop, to enlist all the neighbors to help in return for a small share of whatever was being harvested. Frequently during harvest time, we'd have grapes or berries, some of which went into the wine. Even though I lived in an urban neighborhood, a real sense of community prevailed. If somebody raised hay, it was a given that we all would go and help them bring it in. If it was potato-digging time, everyone would pitch in and help. In return, the farm families shared their food. That's how everybody I knew got by during the Depression. That, and horsemeat and rice rations. We called the horsemeat 'chalk.'"

At the mention of this basic, unappetizing food, even after seventy-odd intervening years, Max's face registers a kind of revulsion. He goes on, "Things for the family continued to spiral downward until eventually, with Dad unemployed, we went on welfare. This was profoundly embarrassing to me. I vividly remember when we got our first rations of horsemeat. This must have been the late 1920s, 1930s, so I wasn't even a teenager yet. I think at the time I still hoped our situation was temporary, that soon Dad would have work and we could eat real meat again.

"In any case, Mother cooked that horsemeat just as she would have cooked beef. In my memory, nobody even commented on how it tasted. It would have been absurd to ask, 'How was it?' because we had no choice but to eat it if we wanted to live. It was a matter of preserving our lives.

"Luckily, though, Mother could cook anything. We ate bear, possum, squirrel, rabbits. If somebody brought it home, Mother cooked it. To go along with these, there were usually potatoes, beans, or corn. The basic crops that farm people raised were our staples.

"The winter I was about fifteen, Dad would sometimes borrow an old, broken-down truck from a neighborhood character named Mr. Stevens, and Dad and I would go to coal yards and ask whether there were requests for coal to be delivered to people's houses. And he and I would deliver this coal for maybe two dollars a ton. The coal had to be shoveled by hand out of a flatbed truck. Ford had higher ambitions. He always said he was going to make his living using his head, not his hands. But I helped Dad all the time with those coal hauls. We'd shovel that ton of coal through a window into somebody's basement, or into a coal shed or bin built on their property for such a purpose.

"Dad just never gave up trying to earn a dollar or two. Once in a while he'd get a regular job. He was a good welder, for example, and he constructed the sign over the Springfield Park Entrance. It was a work of art. It spanned the entrance into the park, and spelled out the words
S P R I N G F I E L D   P A R K.

8

A Summer Job

Eugene Brannon reflects on the way he and his cousins worked during the summers. They sweated plenty to earn a dollar, he recalls. "Even though my dad had a steady job, his wages were low, so I started working at a very young age. Anything I could do to earn a dime or a quarter, I would do. If I got a dollar for a day's work, I was in high clover. Kids won't do this any more.

"But I used to go to the plant where my father worked. They had an outside wash rack there, for washing cars. The company let me use the rack and I'd wash people's cars, clean them really well, and then I'd grease them. Next, I would simonize, or wax, them. It was really hard work, but I got fifty cents a car! On Saturdays, I might make as much as $2.50 for a day's work!

"I was thrilled with the money, but I had more work than I could handle. So one day I called Max and told him that if he wasn't doing anything, he should come on down to my place, and he and I could wax cars all summer. He jumped at the chance.

"So he came down and lived with my family that summer, and we waxed every car we could get and then split the money. At the end of the summer, he bought himself a new three-piece suit. It was a good-looking suit, like a zoot suit, with wide shoulders, wide lapels. It was sharp, and I'll tell you, Max was so proud of that.

"We called that a profitable summer."

9

At Home and
On the Streets

Because there was no money, there were no books, no library, no musical instruments in the Carrs' house. "All my life I aspired to play a musical instrument," Max says, "especially a guitar. I grew up around people who produced hillbilly music. But in our family, music and books were luxuries we couldn't afford."

Asked what a typical family evening was like during the Depression, Max paints a word picture. "After supper, when the dishes had been cleared and washed, Juanita would set up to study at the round pinewood kitchen table. Ford would sit across from her, his books spread out before him.

"Sometime in the late 1920s, Dad bought a brass Aladdin-type lamp. To make it work, pressurized kerosene was funneled into an asbestos mantle. It was a lot of trouble, by comparison with electricity, but we had no electricity and that lamp put out a brilliant light. It was a huge improvement for us. I thought it was great to have that light, because prior to that we'd only had kerosene lamps, and they only had wicks. They didn't give out much light.

"In later years, after we got electricity, Ford and Juanita would do their homework in the evenings while Dad craned toward our Philco radio, listening to Franklin Delano Roosevelt's fireside chats. Mother, too, would listen attentively as she mended our worn clothes, or knitted blankets for the winter months. As for me, I was listening, too, and trying not to let Mother notice I wasn't studying.

"FDR was a true phenomenon. His radio speeches were enthralling. Like families all across America, we wanted to hear what the president had to say. His voice was one for the times. He could do no wrong in the eyes of working people, all of whom saw him as a genuine leader, one determined to meet the needs of America's poor. We believed in him. We truly believed he would do good for us, and he did. He brought about the welfare system, which kept many families I knew during those years from literal starvation."

Meanwhile the radio, so central to American families during the 1920s and 1930s, provided entertainment as well as information. "I wouldn't think of missing Will Rogers' homespun talks," Max recalls. "My mother would be working, preparing for the next day, and Ford and Juanita would be studying, and there I'd be, glued to the radio. Mother and Dad got so upset with me because I wouldn't study. They couldn't say much about it, though, because I brought home good grades."

Glenn and Mary Louise, the youngest two Carr kids, were seven and ten years behind Max, so he remembers them from this period as babies and toddlers. "I wasn't expected to take care of them, or babysit," he says. "Mother handled all that. She was weighed down with responsibility, I realize that now. She never went anywhere.

"But I saw affection in Dad's gestures toward Mother, and the warmth that he would show her." Max seems to gaze into the past, remembering. "He called her 'Ma'am.' That was strange to me. It sounded so formal, but Dad always referred to her as ma'am, even though she was younger than he.

"In general, I sympathized with Dad. Dad never had the money to buy flowers, or candy, or gifts, and since he never had money for such things, he just never developed the inclination.

"In my mind, though, he was considerate of Mother, and respectful toward her. They had friends throughout the neighborhood. We had practically nothing, but they could make a fifty-gallon keg of wine from wild chokecherries or grapes that we'd picked by the roadside out in the country, and when it was ready all their friends would show up.

"It was never an easy life for my parents. After Mother died of cancer, Dad didn't live more than a few months. The truth is, he didn't want to go on living. He probably willed himself to die."

The family's poverty made school a challenge for the Carr children. "I was so embarrassed when I would go to the school gymnasium," Max recalls. "Ford and I played sports, and we certainly couldn't afford tennis shoes, so we had to play in our socks. I had only one pair of long black stockings, and after I'd worn them for a while, the toes wore out. This was humiliating. When we were working out, I'd try to tuck in my socks, to hide the holes somehow, but of course as I ran, my toes would work their way out.

"Soon after Dad was laid off his job," he goes on, "he started getting sick, and then sicker." The family spiraled ever more deeply into poverty and, as the Depression dragged on, everyone handled that fact of life in his or her own way. Mary never worked outside the home. She stayed busy raising five kids and keeping that small house immaculate.

But as their lives became more difficult, Mary worked harder and harder, tending her garden, canning food to put on the table. Okey, meanwhile, became increasingly angry and despairing.

The Carr boys wanted to help their parents however they could. Max says, "I'd go out and work on farms. I would just do any work I could do to help the family. But money remained tight."

"We were poor, so we all had to pitch in." adds Ford. "When I was in my second year of high school, I got a job working in a stock room, and I started earning $15 a week. This was big money, and I'd bring that home to Mom. I was the oldest, so I felt especially obligated."

"When Ford started working and had an income," Max recalls, "he bought Mom a living room set. It included a padded sofa, which was a real luxury. He bought things for Mom that Dad couldn't buy." Only many years later did Max come to realize how that might have affected his father, adding to the older man's feeling of despair and helplessness. "When a man can't support his family, what good is he? I know my father wondered."

The brothers helped their family, but in the larger world their frustration continued to find new expression.

Max says, "I'm not proud of this story, which took place when I was about fourteen. Two older African-American men, Mr. Bell and Mr. Malone, had a shanty down at the dump where they stored copper and iron for salvage. They would try to make a few bucks selling the scrap. At one point, they had quite a bit of copper and iron collected. On this particular day, I'd been to the dump to gather aluminum, zinc, iron—just anything I could collect and sell to scrap dealers for a few cents. This was the only way I had to make money, and I was desperate to make some money.

"But I was taking materials that these guys needed for their livelihood, competing with them for scraps. I didn't have any right to do what I was doing. Now I realize I was actually stealing from them, though that's not how I saw it at the time.

"Anyway, when I went up there, smart-ass kid that I was, I remember Mr. Bell's asking me, 'Why are you doing this? If I was a white boy, I wouldn't be doing this. I'd be in school trying to get me an education.' Suddenly, I wondered what it must be like to be him, but that didn't keep me from smarting off to him. We got into a little fracas. I don't know, maybe he took me by the arm or something. In any case, I resented it, and I resented him.

"A few hours later I told Joe and a couple of other guys in our gang about the incident. That night around dark, I heard them calling for me out in the yard. As I walked out of the kitchen, I picked up a box of matches. It must have been mental telepathy, because Joe was standing there with a can of gasoline. This was a completely unspoken thing. We just started walking toward that shanty and when we got there, we opened the door, threw gasoline in, and tossed matches in behind it.

"Immediately, Joe and the other boys started running toward the clay pits to hide. I ran in the other direction, toward my friend Mike Mylnar's house. The Mylnars had a two-story house, and the family gathered in that little upstairs kitchen. They were poor as they could be, but they always did things together. They made candy, played cards. So I went to their house and sat down and started playing a card game called Tong with them. As we played, I sat where I could see the shanty. I kept watching it, wondering why it wasn't on fire.

"Then, about ten minutes later, the whole thing exploded. We all got up and ran down there, and we saw Mr. Malone and Mr. Bell. I heard Mr. Malone say, 'I'm just trying to make a living until the Lord calls me.' Looking back now, I feel so bad. Mr. Bell was lamenting what was happening, and Mr. Malone said, 'Let it burn, Mr. Bell, let it burn. There's no hope for it.'

"As for my friends and me, our minds were so misdirected. At the time, we were just thinking we weren't going to let these colored men push us around. We even thought the whole situation was funny."

This time, though, some of the boys got caught. Max says, "My friend Joe Barnes was worlds ahead in understanding engines. He knew how to make the positive flow circulation in engines that automotive companies adopted in later years. All cars use this process now. Anyway, the next day Joe was talking to Mr. Bell about this process. Something in the conversation raised suspicions in Mr. Bell's mind, and he said, 'Young man, they going to take you down to the police station and they gots machines that will make you tell what you know.'"

Max says, "We all thought that was hilarious, until the police *did* come, and they took my pals downtown. Later, I found out that when the guys got to the station, Charles Sheffler argued for telling the authorities I'd been in on the arson, too. But Joe, who was a bruiser, threatened to beat Sheffler up if he told on me. Consequently, I wasn't arrested with the other guys.

"At least not that time."

Max's buddies stayed in jail for two days and two nights, but in the end the authorities let them out on condition that they would rebuild the old men's shanty. "The families of the other three boys had to spring for the lumber," Max says, "but my family didn't have to chip in. Thank God. My dad would have killed me. My family didn't have any money at all."

So Max paid with sweat equity. He and his buddies worked together for the next two weeks, rebuilding the shanty. "In the end, it was a much better building than it had been before," says Max. "We really put some heart into the project, and from that day forward, I never went back to take materials from Mr. Bell and Mr. Malone."

10

School and
the Neighborhood

Life on the street might have been rough, but Max's school days were not. He had scores of friends, and even before he was a teenager, he found himself interested in girls. "From grade school on, there was always some young lady that I thought I couldn't live without," he laughs. "When I was about twelve, it was a girl from the neighborhood named Alberta Poukas. Alberta was a small, delicate-looking girl with cropped hair who was always embarrassed because her family had come from Lithuania as immigrants and they all had to learn English once they got here. They lived in a house, though, which indicates that her father must have had a job.

"Alberta entered school the same year I did, and we went through the grades together all the way to graduation. When I was a boy, she was constantly in my thoughts. I was completely infatuated.

"One night, I went to the movies at the Cameo Theatre. Admission was a nickel. I sat down in one of the middle seats and waited for my eyes to adjust to the darkness. When they did, I saw Alberta sitting a few rows ahead, with Phyllis Minor. Suddenly I was overcome with the desire to let Alberta know how I felt about her—but I was far too embarrassed to tell her. So I wrote a note that said, 'Max Carr loves you,' signed, 'The Phantom.'

"I slipped down the aisle on my hands and knees until I drew even with her row. My heart was pounding. I tapped the knee of the man sitting in the aisle seat, and I whispered my request that he pass my note four seats down. He looked startled, then amused—but he did as I asked.

"I hurried back to my seat and watched Alberta open the note. After she read it, she leaned over to say something to Phyllis, and the two of them started giggling. From then on, I had a nickname at school: I was the Phantom. The note didn't work miracles, though. Alberta never became my girl-friend."

All through their teenage years, Max and Ford fought against the resignation that pervaded their world, sometimes by taking foolish risks.

"We were reckless," Max says. "Completely reckless."

"True," says Ford.

The brothers' thrill-seeking repeatedly led to trouble. "We used to go to this one part of the city at night," Ford says. "This was an area where everybody dumped rubbish over the bank, and we'd set the pile afire just for the kick of seeing the fire truck roar up. The firemen would be there for twenty-four hours, trying to put out the fire we'd started out of meanness and boredom."

In fact, the boys were fascinated with fire. Ford reports that there was a house on the corner owned by a lady named Mrs. Nellie Finch. "The house was empty and we knew it. It had a big long porch. We were cocky in those days, and one night we were in a celebratory mood because we had whipped a couple of guys in the neighborhood. So we tore the banister down and set fire to it to make a victory fire."

Max takes up the story. "That's true. Ford and Joe Barnes and I, as well as a couple of other guys from the gang, were hav-ing a great time roasting wieners and playing around. Unfortunately, though, somebody reported us, and the police later came to the house. When they knocked at the door, Dad let them talk to Ford in the living room. I hung out in the adjacent room where, being a smart aleck, I started singing a prisoner song. I was just sure Ford was going to jail. I don't know why I thought I was exempt. I guess because I wasn't the one standing in the living room talking to the police.

"But Dad told the police not to worry, that he would take care of us. And as soon as they left, he damn sure did. We got some of his 'peach tree tea,' as he called it. All that peach tree was good for was his switches. I don't remember ever seeing it yield a peach."

Around this time, Ford was dating a girl named Ethel, who later became his wife. "Well, Mrs. Nellie Finch was a neighbor of Ethel's family," Max says, "and the day after that fire, she came over to talk to Ethel's father. 'These two Carr boys from Roscoe Street burned my porch,' she sobbed. 'I don't know if you know these boys, Ethel, but you stay away from them!'"

"Years later, though," Ethel adds, giggling, "after we were married and all, Mrs. Finch met Ford, and she liked him."

Were Okey and Mary aware of their sons' behavior on the street? "I don't think they were," Max says. "I doubt they even knew about the Roscoe Street Gang. They had to have known there was a criminal element with some kids, an urge that led kids to be unlawful. But I don't think they expected us to be involved."

As year followed year, the brothers continued to skirt serious trouble—but barely. "The Akron paper did a story on the 'Roscoe Avenue Gang' once," Max says. "In it, the reporter talked about the immigrant population of the neighborhood, and how all of us kids were extremely poor. He wrote that we didn't have much parental guidance. However, in our family there was plenty of parental guidance. Ford and I knew the difference between right and wrong. It's just that we usually chose the wrong.

"Even so, the two of us seemed to have a governor, an internal governor, that kept us from going all the way with these destructive urges. We didn't participate in robberies, for example, though some of our friends did. In fact, two brothers in our circle, Herbie and Howard Wise, became habitual criminals and eventually were handed life sentences. I don't know what their home life was like.

"Things turned out all right for those boys, though. When World War II came along, they were paroled from prison to join the military, and after the war, the two of them became prominent union leaders.

"I don't think the guys that I grew up with were really bad, although I can see there's evidence they were. Some of them were plenty strong, and good fighters. Some even became champion boxers. Take Johnny Couvadis.

"Johnny was this Greek kid in our gang who became the state high school wrestling champion. Once when he was in high school, he was visiting a girl in another neighborhood. The neighborhood was rough, like ours, and there were three youths from the Case Avenue gang over there who resented Johnny's being around. So they jumped him. Two of them held Johnny down while a third one beat him up.

"The next day, a carnival was visiting the area, but it was closer to that neighborhood than to ours. Our group decided to go to the carnival and look for the guys who had attacked Johnny. We were looking for revenge. Johnny said he just wanted to fight their leader, whose name was Blackie, in a fair fight.

"So the whole gang of us went to the carnival and sought out Blackie. We made arrangements for a fair fight, and together our leaders laid down the rules. It was decided that the fight would take place on the Kent school grounds. When word spread through the crowd at the carnival about what was going to take place, about two hundred bloodthirsty people left the carnival to watch the fight.

"It was dark on the school grounds. All the people arranged themselves in a circle twenty feet across. Inside this ring of spectators, Johnny and Blackie crouched, facing each other. Johnny got into his wrestler's crouch. He'd move toward Blackie, and Blackie would hit him in the face. Here was a boxer fighting a wrestler and, champion or not, Johnny was getting the worst of it. They came close to where I was standing and the guy next to me tried to trip Johnny. I barked, 'Don't do that. Just let them fight.' But it was obvious that this guy was looking for trouble himself.

"When I confronted him, he threw a punch at me, so we, too, began fighting. Now there were four guys fighting in the circle. I was in good shape during those years. I was eighteen years old, and I was fast. Right then, I was overcome with the desire to destroy this guy, so I kept hitting him in the face with my fists, as hard and fast as I could.

"We fought standing up, and we fought rolling around on the ground. I knew I was getting the best of him, so when I got him lying on the ground I asked him whether he'd had enough, and he said yes. I was relieved to hear it, so I rolled away, and sprawled on the ground to catch my breath.

"Right then, he jumped straight up in the air, and came down with both feet on my face, laying the brow of my eye down over my eye. Enraged, I jumped up and attacked him. Onlookers later described the fight. They said they'd never seen anybody hit so many times. I literally destroyed the guy.

"A few days later, a runner came to our weight-lifting location to tell me that my opponent had not been able to get out of bed for three days, but that he was up now and wanted a re-match. That's when I learned that my opponent was the light-heavyweight Golden Gloves champion of Ohio. Wisely, I declined his offer for a re-match.

"As for Johnny, I don't know what happened to him. I do know that his face was beaten to a pulp. He really should have known better. A wrestler cannot beat a boxer."

Not all crime in urban Akron during the late-1920s and 1930s was petty, as big-time criminals also passed through town occasionally. "When I was a teenager," Max recalls, "Pretty Boy Floyd holed up in Akron for a while. One day he killed a policeman down on Canal Street, and when that happened, everybody in town knew he was in the vicinity. People became really jumpy, especially the police, who immediately started an all-out search for Pretty Boy. Families hunkered down, and people became nervous about being out on the streets at night.

"One night, I was lying in bed around 10:00, just about to drift off to sleep. Suddenly I heard gunshot right outside my window and a deep voice shouted, 'That will stop you, damn you!' I sat bolt upright. *What was that?* Being a fool kid, curiosity outweighed caution. I pulled on a pair of blue jeans as I ran out the front door to see what was going on.

"Right next to our house was a vacant lot, where I had to jump a fence about eighteen inches high. As I did so, two policemen started running toward me, shouting, 'Look out, son. Be careful!' I looked down and saw something lumpy at my feet. It was a man, rolling on the ground and moaning. I had nearly landed in the middle of him. I couldn't see who it was.

"The two cops yelled at me to get out of there. I was momentarily confused. Who was this man groaning in pain? As I backed away, I could tell he was really in bad shape.

"A crowd soon gathered. Later an ambulance came and carted the man away. He had stopped groaning. With that, the police broke up the group, and everybody went home. The next day it was revealed that the man on the ground had been Mr. Ziegler, who lived four or five blocks away with his family. He had a son my age. Now Mr. Ziegler had been shot with a riot gun, and he was dead.

"The story came out over the following week. Apparently, neighbors had seen Mr. Ziegler lurking around the house of some neighbors of ours, the Zarinskys, a fatherless family with several daughters. Nobody could say why Mr. Ziegler had been there, but what *was* clear was that he didn't want to be caught there. One neighbor reported that Mr. Ziegler had been there earlier that same day. Somebody asked him what he was doing, and he came up with a lame story about trying to get grass for his rabbit. Of course, there was grass at his own house. He didn't need to come to an adjacent neighborhood, at night, to get grass. Folks assumed that he had been trying to romance one of the Zarinsky girls, which was scandalous, since Mr. Ziegler was a family man with children.

"In any case, the police were on edge that night. With a nationally known criminal in the area, and with one of their own shot and killed only a few blocks away, the cops were trigger-happy. In the end, it emerged that Mr. Ziegler was just somebody in a place where he shouldn't have been, somebody who ran because he didn't want to get caught there. But as a result of events that night, we had one more widow and several new orphans in the neighborhood.

"In the days that followed, we all assumed Pretty Boy Floyd had left town. But one afternoon, my friend Mike Milnar and I were walking down Lucy Street when all at once Mike pointed to a small, ordinary-looking house and said, 'Did you know that Pretty Boy Floyd is hiding in that house?' I don't know how Mike knew that. Things just got around. People talked.

"The next day, Floyd was gone. I believe he was shot to death in another state soon after."

11

Killing Jesse White

During summer vacation between tenth and eleventh grades, Max did go along with a serious plan to break the law. "I had a cousin, Bob," Max says. "Bob was the son of my Aunt Gertie, my mother's sister, and his sister, Maxine, was my age. We'd all grown up together as cousins. Well, Aunt Gertie probably had the worst judgment, in terms of her relationships with men, of anybody ever born. Mom used to chuckle about it. She'd say, 'Gertie's like a butterfly who flits from flower to flower, and then lands on a pile of cowshit.'

"Anyway, at the time of this story, Gertie had been living with this fellow, Jesse White, for about eight years. They weren't married, and that was scandalous enough, but things actually got worse. Jesse White had been in the house all during the years my cousin Maxine was growing up, from the time she was eight years old. Then, when Maxine turned sixteen, she ran away with ol' Jesse. She stole her own mother's boyfriend. My Aunt Gertie was completely distraught.

"The next day, Bob came to me and asked me to go to Detroit with him, to find his sister and Jesse White.

"'Sure,' I said. 'How do you know he's in Detroit?'

"'I just know," Bob said. 'Are you coming or not?'

"'What are you going to do when you find him?' I asked.

"'I'm going to kill him,' said Bob.

"'Okay,' I said. 'I'll come along.'

"Now Bob had an old, broken-down car, but we had no

money for gas. Bob said, 'Here's the plan. We'll go down to this automobile agency where I work.' He had a job cleaning cars. 'We'll rob the place and get enough money for gas.'

"So that's what we did. We went down to this place about 1:00 in the morning. We didn't have to break in. Bob had a key to the place. We got in there easily, and we sure didn't have wholesome intentions.

"Bob told me not to call his name. So we sneaked in, quiet as could be, and started looking for cash. All at once, we heard a noise. Quick as a flash, we ducked behind this desk. We were trying to figure out who else was in the place. We stayed still, listened, and pretty soon it became evident that whoever it was was also there to rob the place. What a coincidence! Two other guys breaking into the place at the same time we were, making their entry from another part of the building. I didn't have a clue what to do.

"Impulsively, I jumped out from behind that desk and yelled as loud as I could! No words—just a war cry. Those fellas nearly jumped out of their skin, scared to death. They took off and started scrambling out the window. I stood up and shook my fist at 'em. 'And don't come back!' I yelled.

"Then we took the cash we needed and headed for Detroit."

Max says somehow Bob's dilapidated car made it all the way there. "When we reached Detroit, we found a café and wolfed down some hamburgers. I can still remember how hungry I was. Then we parked the car and started walking. We couldn't waste gas on driving around, because we barely had enough money to make it back home as it was. So we slept on the ground in public parks, or stretched out in the car to get a little sleep.

"Of course we were just mixed-up kids, and we had no idea how to find Bob's sister and Jesse. Detroit was a big city. We stayed there three days, walked the streets, drove around a little, and in general made a show of looking for them. Naturally we had no luck.

"On the third day, I said, 'Bob?'

"'Yeah?'

"'Let's go back to Akron.'

"'Ah, hell,' he agreed. 'The two of them deserve each other.'"

12

Hard Knocks

In the Carr home, the financial situation remained grim. Money was tight and the family continued to rely on welfare to survive. Max wanted to help his folks however he could. Since he'd never been afraid of hard work, he didn't hesitate to accept when he was offered a job picking root vegetables the summer before his senior year in high school. "There was an Amish community near Akron, where people had drained some swamps and were using the land for raising beets, carrots, radishes, and other root vegetables. I worked for them for fifteen cents an hour. At five in the morning, we would kneel down in the dirt and hand-pick the grass out of the rows between vegetables. Within a couple of weeks, we pickers would develop abscesses on our knees where the dirt collected. The supervision was very harsh. We were expected to work on our knees and elbows for three to four hours at a time without a break. If one of us tried to straighten up, he would be admonished. I didn't mind the hard work, but I resented the people who expected us to work under these conditions for fifteen cents an hour."

This work lasted for a couple of months, and then it was time for Max's senior year of high school.

Max always managed to keep his street life separate from his school life, where he was a student in good standing. In fact, when he was in twelfth grade, the school found itself with an overload of students and not enough teachers, so Max was asked to help teach the electricity classes. His qualification came from the fact that he could build anything. With materials scrounged from the city dump, he had built crystal radios and one-tube radios, repaired small motors, and tinkered with parts until he assembled, for example, a working pair of skates.

Around the same time, he was elected president of the National Honor Society. He monitored the study halls and helped other kids with their studies. At school, he showed clear signs of leadership.

When Max graduated from high school in 1938, his job prospects were bleak—like everyone else's in Depression-era America. This added to a frustration that was not always vented wisely. One day his impulsiveness caught up with him.

"I had borrowed my dad's car to take five or six of my rowdy friends out to the portage lakes to go swimming," he says. "We weren't drinking. Actually, we didn't drink very much. But we were singing and acting crazy, and for some reason I started driving like a maniac. I passed a car on the crest of a hill without a clue as to whether a car was coming up the other side of that hill.

"Well, apparently some sheriff's deputies had been following me for about fifteen miles while I broke practically every traffic law on the books. I'd been so busy acting the fool that I hadn't even noticed them. When I did see them, I immediately tried to outrun them. In those days I saw the police as the enemy. They were on the other side. There was so much corruption on the force, and police at that time could do anything they wanted to and get by with it. So we kids never would rat on each other, because some day we might be in trouble, and we wouldn't want someone to rat on us.

"It was always a battle, us against the cops. For example, one day one of the guys needed some bicycle tires. We knew of a place over on the other side of town where there was a whole block of used tires, including bicycle tires. We started heading that direction, and then I suddenly thought, *Hey, I don't need to go. I don't even have a bicycle.* So I left.

"I was walking home through the streets of Akron when this police car came by, stopped me, and told me to get in. The two officers started questioning me; they said somebody was stealing tires in that part of town. I kept my mouth shut. I glanced under the seat in front of me, and saw a riot gun there. It bothers me to remember that I had the thought, *What if I should pull this trigger?*"

As he raced along the highway leading from the portage lakes that afternoon, the police followed closely. "Maybe because my friends and I had always been so good at getting away from the cops when we were afoot, I had the idea I could outrun them in the car. Bad thinking.

"I don't know how I avoided wrecking Dad's car that day, but when the police finally corralled me, I got a fistful of tickets. They cited me for six traffic violations, with orders to report to a judge within a few days.

"The judge was pretty brisk in handling the case, and since I had no argument for defense, he gave me thirty days in the county jail. Before they took me away, I gave my dad what little money I had, along with my watch and anything else of value.

"My traffic offenses must have been sizable, because one of the inmates at the jail asked me, 'Did you shoot somebody?'"

Once he was locked up in the cell with other inmates, Max quickly recognized that his jail mates were organized into a hierarchy. "Immediately I was interrogated by the head of this gang. Backed up by a trio of bruisers, he asked me how much money I had, and whether I had a wrist watch or anything else of value. Luckily, I'd left what little I owned with my father.

"Upon learning that I had no money, the gang leader wanted to know if I could get some money from outside. I said no. Seeing that they weren't going to get anything from me, the gang just released me to go into a cell of my own. I remember thinking that I needed to appear as hardened as anybody in that cell, so I consciously tried to mimic Edward G. Robinson, the movie tough-guy. I was eighteen years old, and I was strong. They didn't mess with me.

"However, one inmate did approach me for sex. I thought about decking him, but instead I made it clear that he was barking up the wrong tree. Then I was assigned to the Range Gang. My job was to work on food detail. With the help of a chef, believe it or not, we prepared food for the other prisoners. Now mind you, this was during the Depression, and we were living on welfare rations at home. Here in jail, I was eating pork chops. Ironic.

"After a couple of weeks, I had another hearing before the judge, and this time, my dad had a deputy sheriff intercede in my behalf. The deputy explained that I was the provider for my family because my dad was sick. The judge decided I'd paid my debt to society, I guess, because I didn't have to go back to jail. I was actually supposed to be in jail for a couple of months, but after only a couple of weeks, the judge called me in and asked me if I was working. I said I wasn't, but that I wanted to. He believed me, and he let me out—but what a lot of trouble for that one afternoon of reckless driving.

"When I was released, I walked out into a beautiful summer day. There was no one to meet me, and of course I didn't have a car, so I walked the six miles home. As I did, I wondered what people were going to think of me, now that I'd been in jail. I felt so humbled."

13

Finding Work

FDR had created the WPA program in 1934 as a part of the New Deal, and Okey was eligible for it—but he was too sick to participate. Therefore, Max worked in his place, as a stonemason's assistant. His wages increased 400% over what he had earned picking vegetables—to sixty cents an hour! A couple of months after he started, he was given a ten-cents-an-hour raise, which brought him up to seventy cents an hour. At that point, he was also assigned a helper.

WPA workers were only allowed to work twenty hours a week. The idea was to spread the work around so that more people could have money enough to buy at least *some* groceries for their families. Max says, "I was eighteen years old at that time, and the helper assigned to me was forty-two. At first I worried that it would be demeaning to him to work for a kid. But as time passed and I got to know him better, I realized that he was just glad to have a source—any source—of income. In those days, people did whatever they had to do to earn money. Pride was a luxury nobody could afford."

Max soon realized that, even though he was making a salary, it wasn't enough. He had to work full-time if he was going to get ahead, and besides, the WPA work wasn't permanent. "Within a month of my starting on that project, I was elevated from helper to mason. Even so, the wages were low and I could only land twenty hours a week in shifts. This schedule allowed me time to seek employment elsewhere."

As it happened, Max's WPA job turned out to be even less

permanent than he had thought. "There was a man who lived across the street from us, a grown man with children, who couldn't get on with the WPA. He filed a complaint asking why I, as a kid, could get a WPA job while his family was starving. So they fired me without a hearing! It never occurred to me to appeal on grounds that I was working in my dad's place, and I was supporting the family. I didn't know you could do something like appeal."

When he was deprived of his WPA job, Max's yearning for a better life only grew. "We were just so poor. All my dreams in those days had to do with material things. It was more than just the bike I'd dreamed of for so many years. If there was *anything* I saw that I wanted to have, I had no money in my pocket, no money to buy things with. With this as the fundamental fact of life in our neighborhood, many kids thought they had only one choice, and that was to steal what they wanted, to get money by hook or by crook. People would collect old metal, or sell junk. Opportunities for making money were very limited, so we did without.

"Neighborhood kids who had no parental guidance chose to steal. Most of them ended up in the pen, or were shot. In our family, though, we were lucky enough to have parental guidance. I think the fact that it finally soaked in is what saved me from being ruined. That and the Grace of God."

Lucky or not, Max remained intent on improving his station in the world. At night in the hot, crowded bedroom, Max would study the Sears & Roebuck catalog. "They had all kinds of things in there," he remembers. "I would see bikes, clothes, toys. They even had a house in that catalog, a build-it-yourself house that was just charming. I would fantasize about buying that house. But of course my next question was, How in the world does a person make enough money to pay the $7000 or $8000 one of those houses would cost? It was a complete mystery to me, but that didn't stop my dreaming.

"When I was sixteen or seventeen, I came to realize what a beautiful girl Mildred Duriak was, with her blonde hair and blue eyes, and her goddess figure. Mildred was a member of the Russian family across the street. My hormones were raging, of course, and Mildred soon became included in my dreams about what I would own. I'd picture that house from Sears and Roebuck, and me coming home every night to Mildred."

Night after night, his prayer was the same. *Just give me a chance.*

"I didn't really know what a chance would look like," he says today. "But I knew I would be ready when it came."

A few weeks later, Max heard the Pennsylvania Railroad was hiring. "My friend Jimmy and I walked five miles to the round-house," he recalls. "Word had spread that a few men would be hired as section hands, and about two hundred of us applicants showed up to apply for the jobs. Jimmy and I were standing in the middle of all those hopeful men, most of them at least twice our age.

"Eventually out came the hiring superintendent, and he announced that six people would be hired for temporary positions to last about three months. He scanned the crowd and immediately pointed to one man in the crowd; he gestured for him to come forward. Next he signaled another man forward. I realized that these two men were tall—six feet or better. So I stretched up as far as I could on my toes, and sure enough, when the superintendent's eyes passed over me, I got the nod.

"When I walked into his office minutes later, he started laughing. 'What did you do? Stand on your toes?' he asked me, and I said, 'I sure did. I want this job.' He must have had a sense of humor, because he hired me."

It's a good thing Max wasn't under the illusion that this would be an easy assignment. "Section hands were hired to repair the rails, crossties, and the bed that the trains rode on," he explains. "We would start at five in the morning. The job was back-breaking. We lifted heavy ties manually, and lifted the individual rails that the locomotives rode on. We worked out in the hot summer sun. Consequently, people who held such jobs were tough as nails. Some of the fellows I worked with had recently graduated from the penitentiary."

While working for the railroad, Max started attending night classes at the University of Akron, a local municipal university. He was taking some math classes with the intention of becoming an electrical engineer. He'd always had an interest in electricity, but, he says, "I really didn't understand what it would take to become an engineer. I'd never had any guidance."

After a time, he came to the realization that he wanted a job with a steady company, one in which he could rise through the ranks. Since he was interested in everything electrical, and since he wanted to use his talent for making things, all signs pointed toward the Ohio Bell Telephone Company. He made up his mind to get on with the company.

Max had Wednesdays off from his job with the Pennsylvania Railroad, so every Wednesday morning at eight o'clock, as had become his habit over the months, he continued going to the employment office of Ohio Bell to see whether any jobs had opened up. Week after week, the answer was the same. No new jobs.

Max says, "Finally one morning, the employment manager said, 'Son, I'm not trying to discourage you, but we haven't hired anybody new in seven years.' I thanked him politely, and the next Wednesday I was back in his office. This was 1939. There were no jobs anywhere, and I knew that, but it didn't stop me. Every week for a year, I showed up to ask whether anything had changed."

Then one day, things did change.

"The manager who had been seeing me every week told me I was going to be hired as a telephone installer," Max says. "I think I just wore him down. In any case, I was the first person hired by the phone company in Akron following the Great Depression. After a year's weekly visits, I finally got on as a residential telephone installer. My salary was forty cents an hour."

Max was ecstatic. The work suited him, and he liked it— enough, in fact, that he continued as an installer until he enlisted in the military. "I was so glad to have that job that I made up my mind to work harder and longer and faster than anybody. I used to run up the sidewalk to the front door of each house where I was going to do an installation. I never walked. If I left a tool I needed in my truck, I jogged back out to get it." For as long as he could remember, Max Carr had associated success in life with hard work. A job was a privilege, and he wasn't about to take it for granted, or slack off in any way. It helped that he had seemingly limitless energy.

14

Restless Wandering

In 1943, with war raging in Europe and the Pacific, Max decided to enlist. He had his reasons, as he explains. "First, Ed Hamilton was a guy that I worked with at the phone company. It was Ed's ambition to go through the cadet program and become a pilot. He talked about it all the time, and he described an elite military world, ordered and clean, where the cadets were well-dressed, and even wore white gloves. To me that sounded wonderful, because the only gloves I'd ever seen were work gloves, and because most of the people I saw were grimy."

Soon after starting his job with the phone company, Max met a girl named Margie Warner. "I met Margie while routing PBX, or Public Branch Exchange, a business telephone system, in Akron. We were installing a system at the company where she worked, and I asked her out. Soon we started dating, and I guess you could say I became emotionally involved. She had a nice personality and I enjoyed being with her.

"Not long after she and I started dating, I found out I had a competitor for her affections. It was this guy who had enlisted in the U.S. Army Air Corps, and who was completely excited about learning to fly. All he could talk about was aeronautics, and I could see this impressed Margie—which prompted my natural competitiveness," says Max. "I could just imagine that bastard flying around in airplanes. *Hell*, I thought, *if he can do that, so can I*. So I took a test to become an Army Air Corps cadet. It was actually an IQ test, and I scored 160. After that, I was accepted as a pilot.

"The irony is that, after I graduated, I learned that the fellow I'd been competing with for Margie was in the Air Corps all right, but only as a clerk. I had misunderstood. When I heard he was in the Army Air Corps, I just assumed that meant he was a pilot. That little misunderstanding had quite an effect on my life."

After Max qualified, he was sworn in at a recruiting center in Cleveland, but the military was not yet ready to induct him. All he knew was that he would be inducted on a future call, the date of which was open-ended. As he waited, he was restless, so he and a couple of friends from the neighborhood decided to take a road trip in Max's 1941 Pontiac.

"I'd never been to California," Max says, "and I figured this was a last hurrah for me before I went into the army. I assumed I would have time for an adventure before I was called into active duty. So my buddies and I left, heading west on the Lincoln Highway, and nobody at home knew how to reach me or where to find me."

First the three young men went to Cleveland, and then to Chicago. "We stopped at a 'burger place in Southern Chicago, and we met this young girl, about our age, whose dad owned the restaurant. We told her we were going out west prior to my going into the service. She wanted to go, too! I asked her if her dad would give her permission, and she said she didn't think so—but she still wanted to go.

"We left her and continued driving west. We were trying to make time, so we'd sightsee during the day, and at night we'd just throw a blanket on the ground to sleep. We carried our bathing suits in the car with us, and if we passed a river, we'd get out and swim. We were trying to cram those days as full as possible, because we didn't know what lay ahead. Once we were in the military, we might be anywhere.

"We took turns driving my car along asphalt highways. I remember I liked Denver which, in the 1940s, was a small town.

"When we were coming back from Death Valley, we came upon two girls hitch-hiking from California to Texas. We picked them up and they stayed with us until suddenly, in Holbrook, New Mexico, I began to have a bad feeling about being with these girls. We had brought them across two or three state lines, and I was afraid that could bring us problems. I started worrying about it.

"We stopped for gas and the girls had to go to the restroom. As soon as they did, I started the motor and zoomed out of that gas station. I got to the highway and immediately heard a siren behind me. In my rear view mirror, I saw a car with two state troopers pull in behind me. While I was talking to them, I heard brakes squeal and those two girls we had dumped were already picked up by another car."

The cops hauled the boys in for reckless driving and for peeling out of that station, and once again Max was on his way to jail. He told the lieutenant, "You can't keep me in jail because I'm to be inducted in the Air Corps on Monday. If you lock me up, you're going to have to call the officials." He wasn't going in on Monday, of course, but patriotic fervor was running high in the country, and soldiers were heroes.

"I'm not calling anybody," the lieutenant said.

"'Okay, but I've told you that I'm to be inducted on Monday.' The officer paused for a minute, staring me down. 'Is that true? Are you really going to be inducted on Monday?' He seemed to consider a minute, and then he said, 'I'll tell you what. I have a son over there. I'm going to let you go, if you'll get a couple of shots at the enemy for me.'

"So he let us out and we hit the road again. When we made it to Fort Hood, Texas, I decided to call home."

"Glenn answered the phone and when he heard my voice, he said, 'Where the hell are you?'

"'We're in Texas,' I said.

"Glenn said, 'Well, you've been called to active duty, and we have the state police looking for you in Texas, New Mexico, and California.'"

This was a Friday, and Max was to be inducted in Cleveland the following Monday. He'd thought he was lying to the officer in New Mexico, but now it turned out he really *was* going in on Monday.

The three boys drove back to Akron without stopping, making the trip in two days.

The next day, Max became a soldier.

Sawmill near where Okey Carr (left) boarded with "Devil" Anse Hatfield

Left to right.: Max's father, Okey Carr; Max's uncle and aunts: Ben, Lydia, Maude. Belfont, Braxton County, West Virginia.

Left to right: Max, Uncle Ben, and a cousin, in Belfont, West Virginia

Back, left to right: Eugene Brannon, Lonny Boyce, Francis Brannon, and Max Carr; front center: Glenn Carr. Pine Grove, West Virginia, about 1937

Max as a high school senior, 1938

The newly completed family home at 623 Roscoe Avenue, Akron, Ohio, 1925

The house on Roscoe Avenue today. Max planted the large front-yard trees as a child.

Left to right: unnamed friend, Max, Herb Sorenson. Washington, D.C., 1939

Max in Montreal, Canada, on a trip with friends, 1940

*Job application photo,
Ohio Bell, 1940*

Ohio Bell Training Class, Cleveland, Ohio. Max is in the center, back row.

Okey and Mary Carr,
Max's parents

The Carr family. Left to right, standing: Juanita Boyce, Okey Carr, Mary Carr, Bill
Wells (Max's brother-in-law), Mary Louise Wells; kneeling: Ford Carr, Max Carr

PART TWO

THE WAR

15

Training

Max and his friends got home from their cross-country trip in record time. "I hugged my mother goodbye, shook my father's hand, and headed for Cleveland to be inducted. From there, new enlistees were put on a train to boot camp in Virginia, where the real fun started.

"We wore civilian clothes until we arrived at boot camp, and there we were processed into the military and given a duffle bag and our uniforms. Within days we were shipped to Shepherd Field in Wichita Falls for basic training. There, we were all cadets, all new and green. However, we had been carefully selected as a highly promising group.

"The sergeant began to put us through drills. At one point he stopped and said he couldn't believe that we were reacting to his commands as if we had already been in the military. 'New recruits are usually confused,' he told us, and I thought to myself, *Well, we **were** selected as an elite group.*

"What I really remember, though, is how cold it was in Wichita Falls. We all got sick, because we had to lie on the ground. We thought Wichita Falls was a hellhole. I handled it fine physically, but boy, was it uncomfortable. At four in the morning that bugle would sound, and we would jump out of bed, hurriedly dress, and report, in formation, to a drill sergeant. But in the meantime, the quarters we left behind had to be spic and span, nothing out of place. We always knew the premises would be inspected in our absence and that we'd catch hell if anything was amiss.

83

"Every day we did drills. Marching, formation, obstacle courses, classroom training on military tactics and practices. We had no idle time; we were busy every waking hour. At this point, we had not yet had any training in flying, so no training for the mission we would actually be assigned to. All that had been confirmed was that we would be pilots, but we had no idea what kind of pilots. We just knew we would do whatever the military needed for the war effort. If they needed bombers when we finished training, we'd be bombers. If combat cargo pilots were needed, then we'd draw that assignment.

"This period of our training was pure indoctrination. The military way of life introduced us as inductees to an expectation of perfection, and it introduced me, personally, to an entirely new world, one of order and discipline.

"When we finished this part of our training, the military was not yet ready to receive our contingent of cadets, so it was decided that those of us in my unit would begin attending college. We were sent to the University of Tulsa, where we were able to attend a full semester of classes before we were called up. One of my clearest memories of that time was how our troop of cadets used to march through the streets of Tulsa, singing in unison in order to keep in perfect step. Here we'd come down the streets of Tulsa, and our singing and cadence were so unusual that front doors would suddenly be thrown open, and people would stand watching and wondering what was happening in their town— which was not a military town.

"We stayed in a dormitory at the University, one that had previously been used by some of the college athletes.

"It was in Tulsa that I rode in an airplane for the first time. I remember it well. It was a Piper Cub, a little low-horsepower, canvas-covered airplane. This was just to give us the feel of flying. Of course that wasn't what we would be flying on an actual mission. I trained on that plane, though, and later it was the first plane I solo-flew.

"From the beginning, flying was natural for me. I had no dizziness, no headaches. My eyesight was good, and I felt at ease in the air.

"After Tulsa, we went to Stamford, Texas, where there was

another training facility. Here we advanced through primary training, which was step one of formal aviation training. Aviation training consisted of three parts: primary training, basic training, and advanced training. Each of these categories entailed about three intensive months.

"Throughout our training, even early on, guys were getting washed out of the program for various reasons. The number of cadets who dropped out or were eliminated kept increasing, especially as our training got tougher. There was a constant weeding-out process going on, and we all knew it. The knowledge kept us on our toes. It kept us unsure of ourselves.

"As for me, I didn't want to fail. That was my motivation. So I kept moving through the training and trying to master each step of what I had set out to do. I remember thinking about the embarrassment of failure if it ever came to that. In basic training once, I saw a guy washed out and I wondered aloud if that could happen to me. The other guys in the squadron all hooted. 'If you don't make it,' one guy said, 'none of us is going to make it.' Somehow, this allayed my doubts.

"Since Stamford was the first step in our aviation training, we were flying the least sophisticated military airplanes available, the most basic, a plane known as the Fairchild PT-19, a canvas-covered plane with two open cockpits. The instructor sat in the rear cockpit, and the trainee sat in front of him. We had no radios. It's almost comical to think about now, but we communicated by way of a Gossport System, which consisted of earphones with rubber tubings connected to the headset of the other person. It was strictly acoustical, nothing electric.

"I remember one kid was flying with his instructor behind him, the instructor giving him hell, and the kid got so frustrated he took his Gossport headphones off and threw them over the side of the plane. Needless to say, that was it for him. He washed out the same afternoon.

"At another point during primary training, we all had to take a turn solo-flying the PT-19. We were on an auxiliary field that had formerly been a cow pasture. That's where we were going to do our solo training. I had already soloed and I was sitting on the ground with some of the other cadets and the instructor. We were all watching as this kid, kind of a nervous type anyway, took his turn. He got in the cockpit and on take-off he didn't gain altitude fast enough. Those PT-19 planes had a rear skid mechanism, and this kid was flying so low that he snagged a barbed-wire fence and pulled up a couple hundred feet of fencing. Then it was hanging on his skid as he flew. He was afraid to land, so he just kept circling. Keep in mind we had no radios, so there was no way for the instructor to tell him what to do. I remember that instructor said, 'If I had a gun, I'd shoot the S.O.B. down.'

Max reports that, after primary training, it was on to basic. "We went to Perrin Field in Sherman/Denison. During World War II, most of the flight training took place here in Texas because of the open fields and flatness of the land. Also, Texas was sparsely populated at that time, so there was room for this kind of program.

"At Perrin Field, we started flying more complicated, higher-powered airplanes called BT-13, known as a Vultee bomber, though it wasn't really a bomber. I recall it was a fixed-gear, two-seat airplane with enclosed cockpit. Seats were front and back, as with the PT-19, with the instructor sitting in the rear seat. This plane was an all-metal, fixed-gear, low-wing plane.

"This was the first acrobatic, maneuverable airplane to which I was introduced.

"One day I had taken the plane over the school grounds of Haskell, Texas, and I put it through all these acrobatics, showing off for the kids that I imagined were five thousand feet below, watching, awed.

"Sometimes we would have instructors with us, but other times we would be turned loose to learn the airplane on a solo basis. Occasionally we would lose a pilot that way. Several of the cadets had accidents along the way.

"One thing I recall about the BT-13 is that it wasn't readily recoverable from a spin and we were told that if we got into a spin below 1500 feet we should bail out. I never experienced this particular problem. It was mandatory that, at the end of training, each cadet undergo a test ride to assure that the proper training and goals had been accomplished.

"One morning I was in the flight room when a training instructor came in. We cadets were already aware of the fact that one of our fellow cadets had crashed, but nobody knew exactly where. It was also known that his instructor had crashed with him. On the morning in question, the check pilot came through the operations room and yelled, 'Who hasn't had his test?' This instructor was going to give the test while he looked for the crash site. Well, I immediately raised my hand, thinking that he would be preoccupied with looking for the crash site and wouldn't have time to concentrate on my test. So we went out, with me as pilot. We found the burned spot and hastily returned to the airport to report our findings, and complete my test flight. The only problem was that the crash site we found was not the one we were looking for. It was the site for another cadet, who had crashed about ten days earlier. It had been an unlocated site, so we inadvertently found the site they'd been looking for earlier. But we didn't find the one we were looking for that day.

"But I had passed my test."

From Perrin Field, Max went to Ellington Field in Houston for twin-engine flight training. "I was being trained on the AT-10 to be a bomber pilot, because that's what was needed at the time," he recalls. "I quickly learned that flying a twin-engine airplane was more complicated than flying a single-engine airplane, inasmuch as you had two engines to control. The techniques were quite different. By this time, flying had become very natural to me, a secondary reaction

"All along the way, there was somebody crashing, somebody washing out. In that particular plane, the training in Ellington field concluded the phase of flight training at which point we changed from air cadet to a commissioned officer. I was now a 2nd Lieutenant. One of the things I remember being told at that time was that, just because I had the rank, I couldn't expect respect. I had to *earn* respect. That really impressed me, and I kept it in mind throughout my military career and beyond.

"Following graduation and commissioning at Ellington, I was assigned to a B-26 Bomber Squadron at Barksdale Field in Shreveport, Louisiana.

"That's where the incident of the two left shoes took place."

"At the swimming pool at the Officers' Club at Barksdale Field one day, I was with a fellow officer, a Yankee friend of mine from New York. We were both 2nd Lieutenants at that time, unmarried, and like most young men, we were looking for the opportunity to associate with the opposite sex. Well, two young ladies caught our eye at the pool that day.

"After some rather vivid conversation, my buddy and I arranged to meet them in town, in Shreveport, and that night we caught a ride in. We were to meet the girls at The Brass Rail, a bar. When we did, the four of us got along famously. My friend was a really nice-looking fellow. That night I listened to him talk, fast, with that Bronx accent, really handing these girls a line.

"We had several beers there at the bar. Now liquor was hard to come by in those days, but one of the young ladies mentioned that she knew where we could find a fifth of Four Roses Bourbon. We jumped at the chance. The girls were foxes, very attractive.

"We got a cab to this house and the girls knocked at the door. I couldn't see the guy who came to the door but he had a deep bass voice. We handed him a five in exchange for a bottle.

"One of the girls suggested that, rather than going back to the bar, we should go to her house. We thought that was a great idea, so the girls directed the cabbie out of town. I had no idea where we were going. I thought, *Hell, we might end up in Arkansas.*

"We left the city limits and came to a dark suburb. A couple of blocks later we pulled up in front of a small bungalow. We paid the cabbie, and he left. My Yankee friend and I entered the tiny living room, where there was a radio. One of the girls switched it on while the other went to the kitchen for ice and glasses. We uncorked that fifth and started drinking.

"After a while one of them said she'd gotten sunburned at

the pool, and she asked my friend if he would rub lotion on her back. We were deep into that bottle and inhibitions were low. She whipped off her blouse and he started rubbing her down. In a short time, clothes were piled in different corners of the living room and we were all getting lotion rubbed on us. It was about midnight. Eventually, someone said it was bedtime.

"We staggered down the hall. I saw there was a bedroom on the right, and one on the left. My girl and I turned right.

"About 1:30 in the morning, I found myself lying on the side of the bed, right next to an open window. It was pitch dark. I couldn't see a thing. After a time I fell asleep.

"Sometime later I was awakened by a deep male voice that seemed to be calling right in my ear, 'Mary, I'm home.' He said it twice. Omigod, Mary was my date's name. I put my hand out and felt around where she had been, but she was gone. Without making a sound, I slipped out of bed and made for the bedroom door, but I wound up ducking into the open closet by accident. I fell through the clothes into Mary, who was hiding there. Quickly I backed out of the closet, out of the bedroom, and then turned to hurry through the living room, pausing only long enough to tell my buddy that we had to get the hell out of there.

"That voice in the night had been my first inkling that these two girls were married. Now I knew we were in trouble.

"As I rushed through the dark living room, I heard the front door knob rattle, but the door was locked and whoever owned that big deep voice couldn't get in. That door was within arm's length of me, so I reached down for my shoes, and shoved my hand into one with the heel outward. *If I have to, I thought, I can cold-cock this guy.* Then I heard his footsteps leaving the porch, and the movement of bushes indicated he was walking around the house, to come in the back door. I bent to pick my clothes and another shoe up from the floor and opened the front door.

"I was stark naked as I reached the porch and took out running down the street, with my clothes in one hand and my shoes in the other.

"A block or so later, I looked back, but nobody was following me, so I sat down on the curb and pulled on my clothes. It wasn't until I was lacing on my shoes that I realized I didn't have a pair. I had two left shoes, and one was too small. In fact, I couldn't even get it on. Obviously I'd picked up one of Yank's shoes, but I had no idea where he was. Hell, for all I knew he could have been beaten to death by now.

"With my right foot bare, I walked about three blocks to a highway. I was miles and miles from the airbase. It would sure be a long walk for a man wearing only one shoe. Just then a car came down the highway, and I hailed it. A sergeant in uniform was driving this civilian car. I asked him where he was going, and he said Barksdale.

"As I got in the front seat, I heard somebody chuckling in the back. There was my buddy, sitting behind me. 'You wouldn't happen to have a left shoe to trade for a right, would you?' he asked.

"Those two foxy ladies were at the at the officers club pool the next day—unscathed, I might add. We asked them what they had gotten us into, and they just laughed. They told us their husbands were brakemen on the railroad.

"They were this unperturbed, apparently, because their husbands had never figured out a thing. The husbands had been supposed to be out of town, and they'd come home early, unexpectedly. When they found the doors locked, they just assumed their wives were staying together for company, and had locked the doors for their own safety."

Max was at Barksdale for less than two months, but several incidents from his time there have remained vivid in his memory. One involved a Superman title.

"There was a tradition at the base whereby airmen would compete in athletic events. It was a wide-ranging competition in track and field, including such events as sprints, push-ups, chins, swimming, and other competitive field sports. The reigning champ when I got to Barksdale was this former pro-boxer who, by the way, was dating the colonel's daughter. He was assigned permanently to the support group at the base, and he was very athletic. He had beaten all the previous title-holders to gain the Superman title, which he held for over a year, through numerous challenges.

"One day we were all being evaluated as to our physical conditioning for routine reports, and the guy who was testing me mentioned that I was doing better on these events than the guy who held the Superman title. He and some other guys set up a competition between me and the other guy later that same day. So I jumped in. We went through the whole series of physical events and, sure enough, I bested him on every one. I have to say, I was in the best shape of my life then.

"I wasn't really interested in showing this pro-boxer up. I just competed at the urging of the trainers. The truth is that afterward I had a bad feeling about it. Why? Because this guy was permanently assigned to that base, and he had the status of Superman. It was probably meaningful to him that, among all the personnel at that base, he was the best. It was a mark of prestige for him. And here I was, a transient person who just came through the base and displaced him from that title. It didn't bring me any satisfaction."

Max's training to become a pilot had ended at Ellington, but in Shreveport, he began training for how he would be utilized in combat. To that end, he was learning to fly the B-26, a medium bomber. "The plane was called a Martin Marauder, and it was known as the 'flying prostitute.' Why a name like that? Because it had no visible means of support. The wings were very small, and consequently, at low speeds, there was no great degree of lift compared with airplanes with broader wing surfaces. So B-26 power failures on takeoff or landing could be deadly. For that reason, the planes were also known as 'widow makers.' Once in the air, though, they were highly maneuverable and efficient aircraft. The same qualities that made it hard for these planes to take off and land made them maneuverable in the air."

The B-26 wasn't the only plane Max flew while at Barksdale. He had to log a certain number of hours per month and sometimes, for diversion, he flew the AT-6, or Advanced Trainer. "This was a single-engine, two-seater aircraft. In the plane, the co-pilot sat in line behind the pilot. This was the aircraft that, reputedly, the Japanese copied in designing the Zero. The two look a lot alike. This plane was very maneuverable, even acrobatic. It was a lot of fun to fly.

"After a time, some of us were selected to go into a combat cargo pilot task force, so our training was changed. I was then assigned to Bergstrom to train in the Curtiss C-46 Commando, the preferred plane for transporting cargo. I joined a Task Force, so called because those of us chosen for this group were to address a particular task that was to be accomplished in the war. Our task was to fly combat cargo into the China-Burma-India theatre.

"When I was transferred to Austin, I saw it as good news, because I happened to know that Margie Warner was in Austin, working at the Air Field. She was here because she had a sister living in Austin. She had come to visit her sister and she got a job and decided to stay. When I found out I was coming to Austin, I called her to tell her the good news. She said, 'Well, I'm leaving. In fact, I am going back to Akron the same weekend you're coming.' But she told me about her family members here, and I promised to look them up."

16

Austin

Max was waiting at the train station in Shreveport, about to head for Akron. He had a leave before he was to report to Bergstrom, so he decided to visit his parents. As he stood waiting, he recognized a young pilot that he had trained with at Barksdale. They started talking, and they rode on the train together to Akron.

"When we got to Akron, we parted ways. I headed for Roscoe Avenue and a visit with my family," Max says.

"A few days later, this pilot called me on the phone and told me he was going to get married. He asked me to be his best man. I said sure, I'd be honored. The wedding was to take place at the bride's residence in a fashionable suburb of Akron, and I went there at the appointed time.

"My fellow pilot opened the door and ushered me into the living room where the ceremony was to take place. A spiral staircase descended to the living room from the floor above. Of course, the groom and I were in uniform. There was a congregation of relatives and friends assembled, and in a short while somebody started playing 'The Wedding March' on the piano. I watched the bride come down the stairs. First, her feet, in white slippers. Then the hem of her dress, and soon the bride herself reached the bottom. She was lovely. All at once I recognized her! She was a girl I'd had had a date with before I ever signed onto the military. We had gone to the Trianon Ballroom in Cleveland to dance, just the two of us. A lot of top bands used to play there. Tommy Dorsey, others. We'd had a great time that evening, but on the return trip, the weather was stormy, and as we passed through a small town on the highway, I ran a stop sign. I hadn't seen it because of the inclement weather.

"Well, a sheriff's deputy stopped me and since I didn't have any money to pay him, he took us both to jail. When we got there, I told the policemen I was broke, but that I would come back the next week and pay them a fine. So they let us go.

"And I did go back and pay them.

"After that, I never saw the girl again, until she descended those stairs as a bride. If she recognized me, she didn't let on. I certainly gave no sign of recognizing her.

"That story has a sad ending. After this, I went straight to Austin and reported to Bergstrom. They weren't ready for me, so they told me to take another leave. I said I'd just gotten back from a leave, and they told me to take one anyway. I had no place to go, so I just caught another train back to Akron. When I got to my parents' house, I saw the front door was open. Nobody was home. I remember that as I walked into the living room, I saw a small table to the left of the door. On it was a newspaper, open to the front page. There was my friend's picture. The article said that he had been shot down and killed on his first B-26 bomber flight. This was only a week after his wedding.

"I always wondered how that girl thought of me. I had one date with her, and got her thrown in jail. After I show up for her wedding, her husband is immediately killed. She must have seen me as a real jinx."

Max came to Austin knowing he would remain here for four months, as he gained training as a combat cargo pilot. "It just so happened that, when we were at Barksdale, the need for more combat cargo pilots came up. A group of us was selected to come to Austin for training in the Douglass C-47. While we were in Austin, the C-46 came into wide use, and the rest of my training in Austin was in the C-46.

"When we completed that training, it was time for each of us to be assigned to a combat unit. My group went to a staging center in Indiana, not knowing where we were going to end up. In Indiana, we received the gear that we would need on this overseas assignment. Because of the particular gear we were issued, some of which was tropical, the military clerks surmised that we were going to the Far East."

Sure enough, Max received orders to report, in late January 1945, to a base in Chittagong, in Southwest India, close to the border of Burma—but his orders weren't specific about when he had to show up. His new base of operation, which was on the Bay of Bengal, would be in the combat zone. Max knew that much, and the knowledge didn't particularly inspire him to hurry—especially since, apparently, nobody was expecting him by any particular date.

So he caught a plane from Florida and after making a mid-ocean stop at the Azore Islands, eventually landed in Morocco. "As soon as we landed, I went to the Casbah," Max says with a laugh, "because I'd seen Humphrey Bogart in *Casablanca*."

On impulse, Max decided to take some side trips en route to his new duty. "Since I was in the area, I thought I'd see some sights. I'd never traveled, and who knew when—or whether—I'd get another chance. Being young, and considering the kind of life I'd had growing up, I wasn't reluctant to interpret orders to my benefit."

Max realized he could get from place to place by flying military transports. This was slow, but it worked for the young American seeing the region for the first time. "I went to Cairo and spent a few days exploring the pyramids. Then I decided to visit my brother in Aberdan, Iran."

Ford Carr had enlisted in the army a few months before Max signed up. "He was in the ground troops, assigned to a motor vehicle group driving big army transports. He'd been in Aberdan, the city later renamed Tehran, for almost two years. I got to his unit by way of military transport, but when I asked around for him, I learned he had left just the day before to go to Europe.

"*Okay, I thought. In that case, I believe I'll go to India.* So I flew to Karachi, in eastern India. From Karachi, I proceeded on to Chittagong."

Max had no idea whom he would run into in these faraway places. Besides Ford, he knew several guys from the neighborhood who were here, and also he'd been told his brand new brother-in-law, Harris Philquist, married to Mae Belle's sister, Ruth, was somewhere in the region.

Brother-in-law?

"I got married just before I left for overseas," he explains. "It's a long story.

"Since my friend Margie was leaving Austin just as I was arriving, she made sure I got to know her relatives—including an aunt who was actually a little younger than Margie, an aunt who was more like a cousin. This was Mae Belle Rice.

"My training required me to stay in Austin for three or four months so that I could receive further training in the Curtiss C-46 Commando. My training was intensive, with plenty of time spent in the air and also studying the mechanics of the plane. But whenever I had time off, I stayed in touch with Margie's relatives. The Rices were really warm and welcoming. The father, Dixie Rice, worked for the Reed Music Company, which was an old Austin company that sold musical instruments, pianos, music books. Later, he opened his own music store, and in time he became a prominent real estate broker. In the Rice family were four girls and one boy.

"During the war, Dixie made it his business to be sure the servicemen felt appreciated in Austin. He would have barbecues for soldiers and it became my main source of recreation to visit with the family, all of whom I really liked. We'd play ball, play cards, and just relax. Dixie had a huge, outgoing personality, and he was a great host. Mae Belle's mother, Marie, was the matriarch and center of the family.

"The week before I was to leave Austin to report to a combat zone in India, I had my first and only date with Mae Belle."

Max shakes his head in wonder as he looks back on perhaps the most important decision of his life up to that point, a decision he took without forethought or consideration. "Two days after that date," he says, "on December 31, 1944, we got married."

Today Max acknowledges that, like many young Americans

about to experience the uncertainty of war, he wanted to be married before he went away. "Who knew what was going to happen?" he muses. "Like a lot of guys, I wanted something to hold on to. That way, if we got killed, at least someone would miss us." Also, though he didn't fully realize it at the time, Max felt close to the Rice family. They had provided a home to him, and he might have wanted, in a way, to marry the family. "But of course Mae Belle and I didn't know each other when we married, and a few days later I left and I was gone for almost two years."

But how had this unlikely wedding come about? Max explains. "Jack Starkey was married to Mae Belle's older sister, Louise. He was a glider pilot at Bergstrom, so I knew him both from my training at the base, and from our contact through the Rice family. To tell you the truth, Jack engineered that marriage, and I didn't have sense enough to stop it. What happened was, Mae Belle's mother, Marie, made some comment about how Mae Belle shouldn't marry somebody who was going to go overseas and might get killed. Well, Jack picked up on that, and called a J.P. and we got married right there in the house at 1507 Lorraine. Once it was done, it was done. In our family we never had a divorce.

"I kept thinking I'd made a decision and now I had to live up to it. Also, I knew I'd married into quite a family—very close, but with a lot of turmoil."

There was one other factor that made Max even more committed to this new marriage, however impulsive it had been. Since the first time he had gone to the Rices' house, Max had been aware of Mae Belle's young son, David, from a previous marriage. "The first time I saw David, he was about two, and he was just a beautiful child. Everybody who saw this lively, personable child loved him, and I was no exception."

Overnight, then, Max was a new husband, a new father, and a combat cargo pilot facing hazardous odds ahead.

17

Max Carr, Reporting

Second Lieutenant Max Carr reported for duty at Chittagong Air Base on February 17, 1944. What he couldn't know as he approached his new base was that he would not leave the combat zone again until the day he headed home at the end of the war.

As soon as he and a few other new recruits landed at the base, Max sought out the Airdrome officer and said, "Sir, I'm reporting for pilot duty, Sir."

"Good," barked the officer, and he pointed to a nearby C-46 Curtiss Commando. "Get in that plane. We need another pilot for this mission to Budalin."

So within ten minutes of reporting for duty, Max found himself—portent of things to come—flying a combat mission to Budalin, Burma. This flight provided Max's first view of the Burma Valley along the Irrawaddy River. "As we ascended in that loaded plane, a white marble pagoda seemed to rise out of the ground near the edge of the runway. There was a huge statue of the Buddha right in the center of it. It was beautiful and exotic, and completely different from anything I'd ever seen, but this was only the first of dozens and dozens of pagodas I would see in the months to follow. Also, the land was dotted with white temples as we flew over." Max found the landscape beautiful, even then, even contorted by war.

He had heard all about the Memphis Belle, a B-17 bomber

with a girl's picture painted on the fuselage above the words "Memphis Belle."

"The pilot of this plane had flown ten or fifteen bombing missions from England into Europe. This made all the news back home, and as soon as those missions were complete, this pilot was sent home a hero. I assumed from that that a pilot was rotated home after he reached his quota of missions. I remember thinking, after I flew that first mission, that I'd get my work done in record time. I started volunteering for one or two combat missions a day, so that I'd rotate off sooner. Nobody ever brought up the rotation system, though.

"Finally, after forty or fifty missions, I decided to ask when I would be rotating off. The commanding officer explained to me then that, since we were a task force, we didn't have a rotation policy. In the end, I flew a total of 283 combat missions."

For this reason, as time went on and mission followed mission, he failed to notice the landscape at all, because his entire attention remained focused on the task at hand. That task, from the minute he hit the ground in the China-Burma-India theatre, was to stay airborne and stay alive.

Staying alive was not always easy, and the dangers came from all directions. There was the danger of being shot down, first and foremost. But Max soon learned that a simple mistake could lead to a pilot's death.

And even if a pilot did everything right, danger lurked. "One story has really stayed with me," he says. "There was a red-headed pilot named Logan, a friend of mine. One day not long after we arrived in the area, he and I had identical missions. We were to fly from Chittagong into the Burma Valley. Just for fun, we decided to race. After all, we were going to the same place.

"Logan took off first, with me right behind him. Everything was routine. We did this kind of mission every day, sometimes several missions a day. We were both flying C-46 planes, as usual. I saw there was a thin layer of clouds above us, and I watched as Logan elected to fly beneath the clouds. *Okay,* I thought, *I'll fly above the clouds and gain altitude on him.* Since we were racing to the target, I could outrun him by being above him and putting my plane in a descent to increase airspeed, thereby passing him in the air and beating him to the target. At least that was my plan.

"What happened, though, was that I lost visual contact with him because he was obscured by the clouds. Thirty or forty minutes into the flight, the two of us broke out into a clear sky, and lo and behold, there was Logan below me about two thousand feet. As we had been flying, we had moved into higher and higher elevations in the Chin Hills, a mountainous range between India and Burma with an elevation slightly above 10,000 feet. They're actually a part of the Himalayan Mountains, but the tallest Himalayan Mountains are on the east side of Burma, and the Chin are on the west. At this point we were flying at six or seven thousand feet. The mountainous jungles were dense until they reached the level where vegetation ceases to grow. I saw that Logan was slightly ahead.

"I picked up my radio mike to alert him as to where we were. But before I had a chance to press the button, a tremendous plume of white vapor came out of his right wing and filled the sky for miles behind him, trailing the airplane. I pressed the mike and told him, 'Logan, I think you've lost your gas cap on your right wing.' But before he had a chance to reply, the vapor just exploded. It was a tremendous scene. The sky lit up for miles as that vapor ignited behind the plane. I kept calling Logan and asking if he was all right. After what seemed like an eternity, I heard his voice. 'Yes, I'm all right,' he replied.

"Of course he couldn't see the damage to his plane from where he sat in the cockpit.

"I put my plane in a dive and gained speed so that I could catch up with him. When I did, I flew underneath his plane to assess the damage to his engine and wing. I could see the bottom side of the nacelle, or motor covering. It was burning and it was in shreds. Fearing that the wing would come off and fall onto us, I quickly pulled off to the right. I radioed him and said, 'Logan, you'd better get out of there. Your wing's going to come off.'

"There was only silence. At just that moment, the wing did come off. Logan's co-pilot was a guy named Moon, who had been borrowed from the P-61 squadron, a fighter aircraft whose squadron was operating in our vicinity. Just as the wing came off, my co-pilot and I saw two figures emerge, jumping from the fuselage. They must have been standing beside the open door. We saw two parachutes open. Things were happening very fast. I was trying to fly the plane, so I couldn't watch the carnage, but my co-pilot gave me the blow-by-blow of what happened to Moon. It was pretty gruesome. My co-pilot saw Moon jump out of a loading hatch at the back of the cockpit. As he did, unfortunately he was sucked back into the propeller that was still operating. The plane was gyrating wildly, and Moon was killed instantly.

"The plane crashed into the mountainous jungle as we watched. Black, oily smoke billowed up a couple hundred feet from the crash-site, and we could see two white parachutes settle on the canopy of the jungle trees. I put out a Mayday call so that the British locator unit could pinpoint where we were. We circled the mountainous site while Roger King was triangulating our location. Roger King was the code name for a British locater station that was established to help pilots pinpoint their location when they were lost or needed help. The way this was done involved mathematical and directional calculations of where the radio signals were coming from. There were two locater stations in the area, and together they could read our signal and figure out where we were.

"As we circled, we noticed a flat-looking surface in the vicinity of Logan's crash-site. We thought a light airplane might be able to land at that spot.

"Meanwhile, one of our planes heard us on the radio, and they radioed back that they could see the smoke, so they flew to the spot where the plane had crashed, and we left. After all, we still had a combat mission to fly.

"The two men who had jumped from Logan's plane were the crew chief and the radio operator. We knew Logan could not have survived. Now these two survivors were isolated in the jungle, four or five hundred miles from our base.

"My co-pilot and I completed our mission. It was only later that we heard the details of what had happened. The Allies had sent in a small Liasson-type plane, similar to the later L-19.

Those were lightweight, canvas-covered planes usually used for intelligence gathering and observation. When the Liasson tried to land to rescue these guys, it crashed, too. The grass was high there, and there were reeds. Underneath all that were giant logs, but they couldn't be seen by the pilots, so they crashed against the obstacle.

"All four of those airmen survived, though, both the two who had jumped from Logan's plane and the two who flew the Liasson in to try to rescue them. They were all eventually rescued. The army hired some boats to go up the river as far as they could go. Then they had to go by land, so they negotiated with natives in the area who had elephants. These natives took them in with their elephants, for miles and miles, to rescue the four men.

"This was not a case of our plane's being shot down. Logan's plane just spontaneously blew up. The hard truth is that we lost as many guys to malfunctions and weather problems as we did to enemy fire.

"After the war, I learned that Logan's widow lived in West Texas, only a hundred or so miles from Austin. I knew I should go and see her. I felt I needed to tell her just what had happened to her husband, since I'd been there when he died. However, after that crash, the rescuers were never able to find Logan's remains. Only the back of his neck was found. I couldn't bring myself to visit his widow. Ten years passed. Then one day, I was flying in a reserve group and I met a guy who knew her. He told me she had never remarried, because she believed Logan was still alive. Now, though, he said she was about to be married again. She must have finally given up."

Several times, Max was asked to fly into locations that had been occupied by the Japanese, for the purpose of making sure that the Japanese had evacuated. One such mission remains clear in his memory. "At a briefing session one morning, Captain Osterstock said they had heard that the Japanese had pulled out of one of the airfields at the forward front of the fighting, but they didn't know for sure. So Bill King and I said we would go find out. We were told the airfield was northwest of Mandalay, so we arrived in the Burma Valley and found Mandalay and then started looking to the northwest for this airfield. We spotted it. We were feeling very relaxed, talking about National League baseball, just two guys out flying and enjoying ourselves.

"We descended to five hundred feet and made a traffic pattern to land to the south on that field. We put our wheels down, flaps down, reduced power, and began gliding in to our final approach. Then, just before the wheels touched down, I glanced over to my left and I saw that the apron was chock full of Japanese Zeros, all painted with the big red circles on the wings.

"Whoa. Immediately we firewalled, which is to say we pushed every control full forward and pulled up the wheels, and accelerated away from that runway as fast as we could. Maximum power. But rather than getting up where they could shoot us down, we stayed at the tree line so they couldn't see us. We flew back and told Osterstock the Japanese were still there. We reported that we had not seen any Japanese pilots, but the whole fleet of planes was there. It was clear the Japanese had not pulled out.

"That was the result of some pretty careless piloting. We also had a lesson in the importance of staying alert."

18

Meanwhile, at Home

Max and Mae Belle often joked that nine months and an hour and three-quarters after they married, a child was born.

"I was far away at the time," he says, "and mail was hard to come by in a combat zone. Kathy had been born for a month or so before I heard about it, because mail was so erratic. Letters were infrequent, and they were matter-of-fact. Mail was heavily censored, for one thing, so about all we could do was exchange details. It's important to remember that we were in an advanced combat zone, so communication had to be sporadic. Even so, one thing that has always galled me about the Red Cross is that the Rice family tried to get word to me that I had a daughter, and I never did get that word.

"Eventually, though, I received notice that I had a little girl named Kathleen Marie Carr. I have to admit, I didn't really feel like a married man. I had no idea what the life of a family man would be. And frankly, I didn't have time to think about it. I didn't dwell on it, but there was no assurance I was ever going to make it home. Guys were getting killed around me all the time. But like most people in that situation, I just didn't fret about it. I put the possibility of dying out of my mind.

"The truth is, I didn't really have time to reflect—on home life or anything else. It's a rather hectic life when you're in a combat zone."

19

The Ruby Max Didn't Buy

Another time Osterstock got word that the Japanese had vacated an airfield, and he sent Max and a couple of other guys to find the field that had been described. The men were to confirm that the Japanese were gone. Sure enough, this time they were.

Max says, "While we were sitting on the runway, a Burmese civilian approached the cockpit. He was a young man, maybe thirty, slim, dark-skinned—and he spoke English! He confirmed for us that the Japanese had pulled out.

"He asked me to come with him to see a tribal elder, so I followed him to a cluster of straw huts. I went alone, without my copilot. This young man really had a lot of poise and I felt comfortable and safe.

"We came to a particular thatched-roofed building and we went in the door and the first thing I saw was a Singer sewing machine sitting next to the door entrance. No electricity, but there was the Singer sewing machine. The floor of the hut was bamboo. We walked past the entrance into another room, where I glimpsed a brass bedstead. Again I thought how odd it was to be hundreds and hundreds of miles up the Burma Valley and to see a sewing machine and a modern brass bed in a native hut.

"In the darkened room were four Burmese men, one of whom was quite elderly. I sat on the floor and faced them. They had a pot of hot tea, and they offered it to me. I drank it. The old man could speak English, but not fluently. I don't think the others said a word. I'm sure they were checking me out because

I was the first person from the Allies in there after the Japanese pulled out.

"The old man further confirmed the fact that the Japanese were gone. Then we sat in silence. Eventually, I asked the elder a question. I knew we were close to the Mogot ruby mines, so I asked him whether he had any precious stones. One of the things I'd been doing with my poker winnings was to buy rubies and sapphires. I'd just stick them in envelopes and mail them home.

"The old man said something in Burmese to one of the other guys sitting cross-legged on the bamboo matting, and this guy quickly disappeared. It was dusky in the hut, and hard to see. There was only one candle giving out light.

"Minutes later, the young fellow came back with a small draw-string bag. He handed it to the elder, who opened up the chamois-skinned bag and pulled out a red stone about the size of a nickel. I could see it was a roughly faceted blood ruby. I asked, 'How much?'

"The old man hesitated and then said, 'Many, many rupees.' He repeated it. 'Many, many rupees.' Finally he gave me a number. 'Five hundred rupees.'

"Now mind you, I was playing poker and accumulating money several times a week, and I would bet five hundred rupees on a card hand. But for some reason, in that moment I went brain-dead. I thought, *Max, you know this might be runway glass.* So I decided not to buy it. I left without it.

"Ever since then, I've remembered that ruby and wondered what it would be worth today. "

Something about that experience caused Max to promise himself that he would never, never turn down the chance to buy another ruby. That's a figure of speech, of course. The ruby came to symbolize a missed opportunity. "The ruby I didn't buy," Max says, "might explain why, in later years, Cassandra and I bought gold mines in the Sierra Madre Mountains in remote Mexico.

"But of course, that's a story for later."

20

Chittagong Airport

Max was in the 14th Squadron of the 4th Combat Cargo Group, and the fourteen combat cargo pilots in his group reported for duty at the same time and location as a similar number of pilots in Squadron 13.

"I don't know what to attribute it to," Max says, "but few pilots in our squadron died, while only one pilot from Squadron 13 made it out alive. I knew the guy from Squadron 13 who survived. His name was Malone. A funny thing I remember about him is that he could dislocate his shoulder and make his body into odd shapes. What a funny talent that was.

"A couple of months after Malone and I both reported to Chittagong, he came to my tent and wanted to talk. That's when he revealed that he was the only person from Squadron 13 who was still alive. He was bewildered by that. Why had he survived while all the others died? There was just no telling who would live, and who would die."

Were the guys in Max's group just lucky? Were they more skilled, or steadier under pressure? He says, "All I know is, we went out again and again, and every single time could have been the last. We never lost sight of that.

"Here's what I mean. Our intelligence officer at Chittagong was a man by the name of Captain Osterstock. One day in 1945, he held a briefing in which he reported that Allied troops were engaged in a fierce battle with the Japanese near the road to Mandalay in Burma. The ground troops needed supplies, and

107

the only way they could get them fast was for somebody to fly them in. Osterstock said, 'So I'm asking for volunteers to transport ammunition into that area.'

"A friend and fellow pilot named Hugh King and I volunteered."

Within the hour, Max and Hugh took off for Burma. When they got to the designated area, they started trying to locate the fighting. Intelligence had indicated the hostilities were taking place close to the Irrawaddy River in Central Burma. Fighting was centered in an airfield there, with the Japanese in control of one end and Allied troops—including, in addition to the Americans, Ghurka, Burmese, and Indian fighters—controlling the other.

"We could see the movement of troops and vehicles in the vicinity as we approached," Max says. "As usual, we were flying a C-46 with an open door on the pilot's side. We always took the door off the airplanes to make it easier to offload our supplies.

"That day we were loaded down with ammunition encased in padded bags. That's what the troops needed, so that's what we were carrying, even though, of course, our load made us a flying bomb. We knew we had to get in to the area fast, and offload our supplies to the troops before the enemy could shoot us down. One hit, and we'd explode in the air.

"When we located the Allied troops, we realized there was only one way to reach them, and it required that we fly right over the enemy. In order to complete our landing roll on the Allied end of the field, we had to drop altitude and fly at low altitude, several feet above the ground—but this maneuver put us within easy handgun range of enemy ground-troops. We could see downed planes burning below and in front of us. Fire and smoke clouded our vision, and, gliding down on our final approach, we could hear the chaotic noise of the battle. I don't know how we avoided getting shot down, but somehow we were able to land and get the ammo to the troops at the Allied end of the runway.

"Once we were on the ground, while the ammo was being unloaded, I noticed a British airplane called the Mosquito. It had been shot down, and the wreckage was there by the runway. The Mosquito was a small, fast-moving American-made plane constructed of laminated wood. British pilots had been flying the plane in that area. I hadn't seen one before, but I was curious about how it was made. Since I wasn't needed to unload the cargo, I went over to inspect the Mosquito, and I found this wrecked plane had a low-frequency radio that was still intact. So with basic tools obtained from our plane's kit, I took the radio out of the plane, along with the plane's battery, and carried them back to Chittagong with me. I thought it would be fun to hook it up so the guys and I could listen to the radio in our basha. It's pretty amazing to reflect that I was curious enough about that Mosquito to go over and inspect it in spite of impending danger. I had to wait anyway, while the plane was being unloaded.

"As soon as I got that radio on our plane, we took off fast."

When Max returned to the base in Chittagong, he hooked up the radio to the battery, and sure enough they got a pretty clear signal. "My buddies and I listened to Tokyo Rose on that radio. She had a sultry voice, and she would put out this propaganda telling listeners that the Allies were losing, and inflating the victories of the Japanese. Her broadcasts were designed to make us all homesick, but I don't think it worked—at least with anybody I knew. What it really created in my mind was animosity. She was a traitor. But she had this great voice, and they played American music along with her broadcasts, so we all listened."

In Chittagong, Max and his fellow pilots lived in thatched roofed huts called bashas. The bashas had bamboo flooring, and each soldier had a cot and a footlocker. "The bashas housed two soldiers each," Max says. "We were in swampy, low-lying country surrounded by jungle. On one occasion, somebody killed a five foot long King Cobra about a hundred feet from our basha. The area had another venomous snake, called a krait, so we were always cautious about where we walked.

"We hired basha boys, who were local men who picked up our clothing, did our laundry, and generally looked after us in our basha. Hugh King and I shared a basha. Our basha boy was named Abdul.

"Abdul was about five-two, really dark-skinned, thin. He was probably in his late twenties. I knew he had a young family, and I always tried to be generous with him. I remember being touched one day when Abdul brought me a sack of tropical fruit. Here he was only paid a few rupees a day, and he was bringing a gift to me.

"Well, one day Abdul came to me and he said, 'Sahib, I have a request.'

"'What is it?' I said.

"And then he asked if he could take off an hour early.

"'Of course,' I said, and asked what he needed to do.

"'I need to bury my son,' he replied.

"'Take as much time as you need,' I said. I was so taken aback.

"But the next morning, he came back and started work at his regular time.

"Sometime after that, our unit received our orders to transfer to Myitkyina. I wanted to give a gift of parting to Abdul. I had a pair of very fine quality leather boots made of exotic leather. But I didn't wear them, so I gave them to Abdul.

"But he said, 'No, no, Sahib. I can't take these.'

"'Why not?' I asked him.

"He looked crestfallen. 'They will put me in jail,' he said. 'They will say I stole them.'

"So I gave him a signed, handwritten note saying that I had given the boots to him. He finally took them, but I don't know whether he ever felt able actually to wear them."

Another kind of mission Max flew was called a drop mission—meaning a mission wherein pilots would go into a hostile area and drop supplies without attempting to land. "There were two ways to complete this type of mission," he explains. "One was to attach the supplies to parachutes and let them float down. The other was to pack the supplies in padded containers, so that they could be thrown overboard and survive the impact of hitting the ground."

The complication came when Allied troops were fighting very close to the enemy. In such circumstances, pilots couldn't risk letting the supplies float to the ground via parachutes, because they couldn't control where the supplies would end up. Instead, they had to get right over the Allied troops before they dropped their load.

Hugh King was perhaps Max's favorite flying partner. Sometimes Max would pilot and Hugh would be co-pilot, and other times they would reverse roles. Together, the two had repeated missions. One memorable day, they took off on a drop mission to an area near the river, north of Rangoon.

They arrived at the battle site and located the Allied troops. They could hear the artillery below as they lined up about a hundred feet above the ground for the drop run over the Allied position. As they were completing their drop out of the cargo hatch, suddenly the ground below and in front of them exploded, throwing a shower of dirt and stones up towards the belly of the plane. "My first thought was that a shell had hit right in front of the plane, but before that thought was fully formed, another big explosion on the ground brought dirt and rock up almost to the level of the plane itself. *What a coincidence*, I thought. And then it happened a third time.

"I craned my neck to look above us, and there I saw a Japanese Betty, trying to bomb us out of the air. The Japanese had two main planes. The Betty was a bomber, and the Zero was a fighter-type aircraft. Well, we saw this Betty, but we couldn't return fire, because the only arms we had were our portable tommy gun and one 45-caliber sidearm. Our only choice was to try evasion tactics.

"We took one look at each other, pointed the nose of our aircraft to the sky, and shot into the clouds as fast as we could gain altitude. We disappeared into clouds and smoke, and we managed to dodge hits until we could lose the Betty.

"What I remember most clearly about that was the experience of knowing we were under attack, but being unable to figure out where the explosions were coming from. Not from shelling on the ground below, as we originally thought, but from above us.

"It's not easy to remain oriented in circumstances like those."

But Max had always had good instincts, and in Chittagong those instincts remained focused on how to avoid being shot down or bombed. When he was on a mission, his eyes were always open. He stayed on alert. In these most harrowing of circumstances for a pilot, though, Max doesn't remember being afraid. "I never had time to be scared. I was too busy flying the plane and checking off the tasks that needed to be done. My mind didn't have time to think of the perils, which was just as well. I couldn't let myself think about danger."

The reason the combat cargo pilots were vulnerable both from sky and ground when they flew was that they often flew extremely low. "Our pilots would leave in the morning and just never come back. We never knew what had happened to them."

One such story still haunts Max. "We played poker almost every evening, and one night a young man that I didn't know sat to my right at the table. He was really nice-looking, with curly black hair and a big grin. We liked each other immediately, and we seemed to bond that evening. He took out his wallet at one point and showed me a picture of his wife and two young children, just babies. His name was White. He was a pilot in another squadron.

"The morning after that game, he took off in a C-46 with a load of oil drums full of gasoline. On take-off, his engines failed and he crashed about three miles from the end of the runway in the dense jungle. Those jungles were thick with vines and trees, animals and snakes.

"A couple of guys who were manning an aircraft battery near our airport took off and ran through the jungle to reach the site of the crash. Amazingly, the plane didn't catch on fire. But the oil drums in the back rolled forward, crushing White and killing his co-pilot."

White wasn't dead, so the guys hauled him out and took him to our field hospital.

"The next day I came across one of the nurses from the field hospital. This woman was seasoned. She had seen it all. But that morning, she was in tears, and I asked her what was wrong. She said she was crying because of how White's mangled body looked. He had swelled up to twice his size. Very soon, he died.

"I still remember what a nice-looking young man he was, with a wife and two kids to come home to. But he never made it home."

Being an American combat cargo pilot during the war was arguably more hazardous even than being a fighter pilot. Max explains, "At least the fighter pilots were armed as they flew into the fray. Fighter pilots were charged with engaging enemy aircraft. They had machine guns mounted on the planes, and they would try to shoot down enemy aircraft, and strafe objects and people on the ground. Bombers, by contrast, would carry a load to use in destroying enemy targets on the ground. But they, too, had machine guns for protection against enemy aircraft.

"Both bombers and fighter planes had a means of protection plus they conducted their missions at altitude. Then they would return to the bases."

The added hazards faced by combat cargo pilots, whose planes had no fire power, made it necessary for fighter pilots to provide air cover during certain missions—or at least it was supposed to work that way. "In our war zone, it didn't always work out like that. Our fighter protection was provided by the British. But the truth is, we didn't have much air cover when we flew combat flights. It was always a source of resentment among combat cargo pilots that we were expected to fly no matter what the weather, and no matter the circumstances. Hell, we expected it of ourselves. For sure we never cancelled a flight because of weather. But either through miscommunication or executive decisions not to fly at certain times or in certain conditions, there were plenty of occasions when we would fly combat missions through enemy territory, and fighter cover would never be there.

"Because of that, we came to believe we couldn't count on fighter cover. We adopted the method of ground-hopping, or hedge-hopping, which meant we flew so low we barely cleared the trees. That made it harder for the Japanese fighters to sight us.

"I was young and reckless, so I found it really fun to fly low and then pull the airplane up in order to miss the trees. I've often wondered whether some of the pilots who went out in the morning and never came back might have crashed while hedge-hogging. We had to do it that way to avoid detection, but we knew it was dangerous—though we never talked about it among ourselves. In a way, it was exhilarating and fun, and we thought we were invincible. After all, we were young.

"That's what made it such a shock when, again and again, one of us would disappear and never be seen or heard from again. Those guys just vanished."

Poker

Obviously, in circumstances of danger and constant vigilance, the Allied soldiers had to find ways to divert themselves during off periods. "A lot of the guys found diversion through drinking, but I didn't want to do that," says Max. "I really felt the need to keep my reactions as sharp as possible. I felt I couldn't entirely let my guard down and still keep my edge. I didn't want to risk having my flying skills diminished or my reactions blunted by having a hangover on the day after a drinking party."

The soldiers were provided with liquor and beer rations, but Max just hoarded his in his foot locker.

So what did he do to relax?

"When I was first inducted and I was riding on the troop train to my first training station, somebody pulled out a deck of cards and we started playing Penny Ante. I had played poker with my gang of friends growing up, but always for small stakes. After I got to Chittagong, though, the guys would play at night to ward off boredom. I was either pretty skillful or pretty lucky in those games, because I started winning money a little at a time. By the time I came home after the war, I had a nice nest egg. In fact, that money was enough to enable me to build my first house in Austin. I built it with my own hands but I bought the supplies and materials with money I'd won playing poker during the war.

"Don't get the idea, though, that I'm saying poker-playing is the way to earn a living. In fact, when asked for my advice about how to gamble, I have a two-word answer:

"Don't start."

21

Side by Side with Ghurkas

Most American newspaper and newsreel reports during the war were centered on the European and Pacific Theatres. Less was known of the China-Burma-India front. In part, this may be because it was never what is known as a *theater of operations*, which is to say there was no overall operational command. Command was split among Britain, China, and the United States, with U.S. Forces under the command of General Joseph Stilwell.

"We called ourselves the forgotten front," Max says. "We had no naval support even though we were right on the ocean. Air protection was erratic at best. Nobody ever talked about us. Nobody seemed to know what we were doing in Burma—which was driving the Japanese out of the country, starting at the north and moving south, toward the ocean. Clearing the Burma Road."

In December of 1943, General Stilwell moved to capture Myitkyina through an offensive in Northern Burma. In this effort, the Allies were not fighting alone. Because of a long ago, far-reaching treaty with the British, the native Ghurkas of northern India (what is now Nepal) were side by side with the Allied troops.

Ghurkas were formidable for their stealth, and for ruthless accuracy with their traditional weapon, the Khukri. "A Khukri is a curved knife like this," says Max, holding the one he brought back after the war. "The legend is that a Khukri has never been broken in battle."

Max heard repeated stories about Ghurkas as fierce fighters.

"We were told that the leaders of the Ghurka squadrons had become leaders because they'd accumulated the most heads. They would take all their clothes off and infiltrate the Japanese lines and behead the Japanese. The leader of the squadron had sixteen heads, so he was in charge.

"They carried their knives in their scabbards, but I never saw one draw his knife. That's because if they drew their knives, they had to draw blood, even if they had to nick their own arms."

Max describes Ghurka soldiers as strong and active, with a stocky build. "They were short, maybe 5'6" or 5'7", dark skinned, very muscular. They came out of the mountains of northern India, and of course they were not a learned people. They wore uniforms of khaki trousers and shirts supplied by the British. I remember two scenes in particular involving the Ghurka soldiers.

"Once I flew into a field and three Ghurkas had captured this Japanese lieutenant and two lower-ranked Japanese soldiers. I was amazed that they hadn't killed them, but in any event, they brought them to the field where I had just landed during some of the heavy fighting. We'd unloaded my cargo, and the Ghurkas wanted me to fly the Japanese prisoners of war, along with their Ghurka guards, back to Chittagong to the British intelligence people.

"I agreed, and during the flight I kept thinking, *I wonder why they haven't killed them?*

"This Japanese officer was very neat, trim, well-uniformed, but what really struck me was that his demeanor was completely calm. The other two prisoners were nervous, but he remained nonchalant and impassive for the whole trip, smoking a cigarette, never speaking, just calmly going where they told him to. I was amazed at this, since he was being held by Ghurkas, with their swords and their history of beheading people."

When they weren't fighting, the Ghurka soldiers were helping with the heavy lifting. "They worked hard. When we'd fly into grass airfields in the vicinity of the fighting, Ghurka squads would unload our cargo. We'd set our plane down on a field carved out of jungle, and the Ghurkas would run out to the plane to unload. One day a young Ghurka came racing out to the plane. He was going to beat his friends. But the props hadn't stopped, and he ran right into the whirling propeller. Of course it killed him, but I was amazed that his fellow soldiers in the squad just ignored him. They ran up and started unloading cargo as if nothing had happened. That soldier lay twitching on the ground, and none of them even glanced down."

The 10th Ghurka Rifles, arguably one of the most celebrated units of the British Army, received nineteen Battle Honors for the Burma Campaign, the most of any British Army units in the Pacific Theatre of War. The Ghurkas represented the British Army at the formal surrender of the Japanese Army in Burma in October 1945. Max's squadron flew them their supplies, enabling them to accrue this distinguished military record.

—KEVIN MCKENZIE
Military Historian

22

The C-46

The Curtiss C-46 Commando, largest and heaviest twin-engine aircraft to see service during World War II, was originally designed in 1936. By 1941, it had been converted for use in transporting supplies to troops fighting on the ground, especially in the Far East. With its 108-foot wingspan and a design load capacity of ten thousand pounds, the C-46 could haul more than its close cousin, the C-47—and for this reason, the Commando played a vital role in winning the war. Its huge cargo capacity and extensive range made it ideal for the vast Pacific and China-Burma-India campaigns, including the dangerous flights over the Himalaya Mountains, "flying the hump."

However, the C-46 could be unwieldy, and its engine required inordinate care and attention. Aeronautics was a new science in those years, and a nation at war had to train pilots who could fly in hazardous conditions and who could also, when the need arose, figure out how to do engine repairs—in enemy territory, sometimes in the dead of night, often while being shot at, and usually without parts or instruments.

On combat flights the planes were at times overloaded by fifty percent, carrying up to 15,000 pounds—including enough fuel to last for the entire flight. Cargo included fuel, ammunition, light artillery, supplies, aircraft parts, and even, occasionally, livestock. In addition, combat cargo pilots carried military personnel, many of whom were wounded, as they were transported to where medical care was more readily available. The pilots had to haul as much as they could and still manage a sensitive, controlled ascent, but the extra weight could make take-off shaky—and extra weight also made it harder to gain altitude once the plane was in the air. Combat cargo pilots learned that the planes would do more than they were designed to do, but that in the process, pilots lost a margin of safety.

Gradually, as the fuel was expended, the planes' loads lightened. When they reached their destination, the flyboys offloaded cargo to the waiting troops and flew empty planes back through treacherous mountain passes, just as they had come.

It didn't take Max long to learn the drill.

"I was flying in the Chin Hills with a pilot named Hoover. We were on a mission from Chittagong to Upper Burma, and we were plenty high in the Chins.

"Hoover and I were making our descent into the Burma Valley to deliver supplies and ammunition to troops fighting on the ground in the region. We usually cleared the Chin Mountains with a good bit of altitude, so I'd say we were flying at about 14,000 feet.

"As I've said before, the maximum design load for that airplane was 10,000 pounds, but during combat we often carried 15,000. Things were going fine until we cleared the mountain and started our descent. All at once our plane just stood on its nose. It was on an acute angle of descent, an almost vertical dive. We couldn't tell what was happening, so we made a quick scan and realized that our flaps were in full down position. These flaps are designed to facilitate a quick descent, but you sure don't want them down until you're ready to land. All we knew was that we were unable to restore the flaps to normal position.

"We really had to think fast. We were in a very rapid rate of descent as the seconds ticked by. We applied full power to the engines to maintain the plane in a somewhat steep glide, but we were still heading down rapidly. There was nothing but jungle below us, for as far as we could see in every direction. The plane was about to crash into a jungle thick with tropical trees and vines. Our only hope was that we could put that plane down in the jungle and survive.

"Of course, we always had the option of bailing out, but

before we had fully considered that, so help me God, we spotted a clearing ahead. From our altitude, it looked like it was the size of a postage stamp. This clearing seemed almost like a mirage.

"Whatever decisions we made had to be made in a hurry, because we were going down fast. There was a chance we could land in this tiny clearing, but believe me, it was a long shot. We would get one chance, only one, at landing our overloaded C-46 in this clearing. With a fifty percent overload, there'd be no fly-around if this attempt failed.

"We decided to make a straight-in approach, because we didn't have lift enough for a regular landing. So we plopped that C-46 down on the small grass field, and brought it to a screeching halt. We just dropped out of the sky into that field. Any further distance would have meant we couldn't make it. As soon as we landed, an American Lieutenant on the ground came out of cover and told us the Japs were making daily runs on this field.

"Quickly we threw out our cargo onto the ground and began to assess the damage to our plane. I crawled up into the fuselage of our plane to check the flap control cables. I found, 'way back in the tail of our plane, that the yoke—a round piece that enabled the cables to keep tension—had broken off. This explained why we couldn't control the flaps.

"By coincidence, another C-46 had been shot down and the wreckage was at the perimeter of this clearing. The wrecked plane had an intact cable yoke, and I removed it and installed it in our plane. We had to work really fast because of the constant threat of Japanese air attacks on the field. As soon as I finished, we could control the flaps on our plane. We were in the middle of a combat zone—not the ideal circumstances for aircraft repair.

"I had thoroughly studied the aircraft maintenance manuals, and that surely came in handy as I replaced the control pulley on our plane with parts from the wreckage. Our mechanic was no help. In fact, he seemed bewildered. Growing up and making something out of broken pieces I found at the city dump was now paying off. I remember being calm and focused while making the repairs. Improvising was something I was always good at.

It focused my mind to realize enemy planes were expected at any time to make bombing raids and to strafe the field where I was making the repairs.

"But Hoover and I, and our crew, got out of there as soon as I had the yoke replaced and functional. I probably should have been relieved. After all, we had narrowly escaped disaster once again. But to me, it was all in a day's work."

23

Days and Nights at War

Living with constant danger, sleep-deprived, and caught in an endless loop of fight or flight, Max and the other combat cargo pilots at Chittagong occasionally sought diversion. Their poker evenings provided that and, occasionally, adventures came along with a mission.

Take the time when Max and one of his fellow pilots, Lt. Hoover, received orders to fly some material to the small outpost of Cox's Bazar, an area on the Bay of Bengal known for having the world's longest beach. At 120 kilometers, the Cox's Bazar beach boasts miles and miles of golden sand beneath towering cliffs. The surf there is mighty, and the area is replete with Buddhist temples. The outpost was located 152 kilometers south of Chittagong.

"It was early in the morning, before daybreak, when we took off," Max recalls, "with a crew consisting of Hoover and me as co-pilots, and a radio operator, and a mechanic. Our mission was to deliver equipment and supplies to this out-of-the-way military contingent. It would be a relatively short flight, not dangerous. All in all, a cushy assignment.

"We got to Cox's Bazar, landed in a small grass field, made our delivery—and then decided we were in no hurry to get back to our base. We wanted to do some sight-seeing. Military personnel there loaned us a jeep and the four of us took out to explore the coastline along the Bay of Bengal. We must have driven south on the sandy beach for the better part of an hour. There was nothing but tropical jungle along the shoreline as we neared

122

the border with Burma. We were having a good time, feeling light-hearted. As usual, I carried my 45-calibre automatic pistol. But something interesting happened on that little jaunt, something that led me to put the gun away for good."

The Bay of Bengal had a beautiful beach running right up to dense tropical jungles, which in turn climbed up into mountains. "I stared up at a seventy-foot cliff only a hundred feet from the shoreline," Max says. "It was so beautiful. We decided to go swimming."

The four young soldiers swam in the Bay, relaxed for once. Max remembers it vividly. "The shore was sandy. I could lie back in shallow water and see blue sky above and tropical trees edging beautiful beaches with fine light brown sand, like that of an expensive resort in Mexico. We found we could walk a quarter of a mile out into the bay before the water reached as high as our shoulders. Then, when a big wave would flow in, it would pick us up and float us eight to twelve feet high. It was fun being buoyant when those waves picked us up, and before long I had ventured away from the others. The water was up to my neck. I wanted to be as far out as I could so the buoyancy would cast me that much higher into the air. Every dozen or so waves, a big one would break.

"Soon I saw this huge wave coming in, and I thought, *This'll be great.* I waded out until the water was up to my chin, and I looked seaward. Bright sun shining through the high oncoming wave towering in front and above me made the waves translucent, and gave me an opalescent green view of sky through water.

"Because I was drinking in that view, I almost missed what was coming toward me from a couple hundred feet to my right. An enormous white shark was approaching in the top of that breaking wave. I saw that just about the time the crest of the wave broke, the shark would be right on top of me. I gritted my teeth and steeled myself for the bite from its enormous jaws.

"My thoughts were clear. How peculiar to be standing there looking above me through the water at the shark that would be the cause of my death. I was eye to eye with him.

"I closed my eyes and thought, *This is it.*

"The wave broke over me and I was cast high up in the swell of this wave. When I came down I was still in one piece, much to my surprise. I looked around for the shark, but I didn't see it.

"I swam back to shore in record time. Another day, another near-miss. But I never swam in the Bay again."

The four young Americans stood on the shore, catching their breath after their eventful swim when, Max says, "We saw a completely wild-looking native approaching, walking with his feet in the water, wearing only a loincloth. His bush of black hair stood on end. In his right hand he carried a machete. He looked truly ferocious, a wild man. Not knowing what to expect, I thought, *Well, if necessary I have my 45, and I could shoot him.*"

Shoot him in the back? No. It came over Max how much he would hate to kill this unspoiled native man from the jungle. "The four of us stood still, staring at him as he walked within ten feet of us, his eyes straight ahead. He never even glanced at us, but we couldn't stop watching him. He approached that beautiful seventy-five foot cliff I had noticed earlier. A rope was hidden there. He went straight to it and shimmied up the cliff skillfully, with his machete clinched in his teeth. When he got to the top, he disappeared into the jungle.

"After a brief discussion, we decided we'd be brave enough to find out where he'd gone, and maybe see some wild elephants. There were elephant droppings everywhere. Also, although the area was made up of foothills of the Himalayan Mountains, it was still at sea level. In these tropical jungles, we knew there were Bengal tigers and myriad other wild animals. The idea of seeing rare animals in the wild spurred us on as we followed the native man up the rope to the top of the cliff, found a path, and started trekking up the mountain slopes."

This was a tropical climate, so heavy foliage made slow going for the Americans. But, says Max, "Sure enough, we kept seeing elephant droppings. We'd walked for eight to ten minutes when I almost stepped on a jungle viper. I pulled my 45 out of the holster and emptied it, missing the snake with every shot. Finally I picked up a stick and killed the snake.

"Now I had two reasons to ditch that gun. First, if I'd perceived a threat, I could have shot the native we saw on the beach, which would have been a real shame. And secondly, when I really needed the damn thing to kill that snake, I never once hit my target. I figured that if I wasn't any better shot than that, I might as well put that .45 in my footlocker, and never use it again. So that's what I did. From then on, I carried a Thompson sub-machine gun, which I knew I'd never use unless absolutely necessary."

24

Myitkyina Field

The Allies' offensive in Burma was going well, according to reports, when Max and his fellow pilot Hoover flew a mission into Central Burma. After they'd completed their mission, and while their plane was still parked, two British intelligence officers approached them and said, "We hear from radio contact that the Japanese have pulled out of Rangoon. Do you know if that's true?"

"I don't know," said Max. "Get in the plane and we'll fly over and find out."

Max, the co-pilot, crew chief, radio operator, and the two British Intelligence officers flew to Rangoon to see what they could see. There, they spotted the Japanese airfield, and they flew low enough to see who was still around. Written in white paint on the roof of one of the hangars were the words "JAP GONE."

Max and his colleagues landed and taxied up to the hangars. "Nobody was inside, and nobody was shooting at us," Max says, "so we assumed the radio information we had received was accurate. The Japanese were indeed gone.

"We saw disabled Zeros on the field, and also some land vehicles. One of them was a jeep, so four of us got in and started the jeep. We headed toward the downtown area of Rangoon to see what was there. There were no Japanese personnel in sight. The streets were completely deserted. We drove all the way down to the wharf area, where the Irrawaddy River meets the Bay of Bengal. Along the way, I saw dozens of large white pagodas. The pagodas were intact, but there were no people in sight. All the other buildings in the downtown area, though, had been pock-marked with bullets from strafing by Allied planes.

"I saw only one person in the streets that day. It was an elderly Burmese woman, stark naked and wandering aimlessly. Her hair was unkempt, and her eyes were blank. She seemed completely unaware of our presence. Other than that, there was no human being in sight.

"I found it so peculiar that this one demented woman was the only Burmese person visible anywhere.

"The British Intelligence officers requested that we leave them at the site with nothing except their radios. We complied and drove back to the airfield, boarded our plane, and flew back to Chittagong. It was only later that we realized that the six of us were the first Allied military personnel to arrive in Rangoon after the Japanese had pulled out."

Once Burma was secured, the Allies mission changed. Max's base was soon moved from Chittagong, India, to Myitkyina, Burma, on the banks of the Irrawaddy River. Now they were charged with flying in supplies for Allied forces fighting in China. "Our mission now was to drive the Japanese out of China. That's when we started flying into China. But to get there, we had to fly several hundred miles over the Himalayan Mountains into the southwestern part of China, where the fighting was then taking place. This meant that cargo would need to be flown into China from Myitkyina Field, Max's new home base in central Burma. It also meant Max and his fellow pilots would be flying over and through the tallest peaks of the Himalayan Mountains as they delivered supplies to soldiers fighting throughout China.

Many of these missions were flown into and out of Dum-Dum Air Base in Kunming, China.

Max knew his new assignment would call for greater skills as a pilot. "Up to now our main peril had come from enemy planes that wanted to shoot us down. To counter that danger, we'd had to learn to fly low, stay alert, and evade detection. When worse came to worst, we had to be able to dodge enemy fire. Beyond that, it was a just a matter of fate.

"But now, with this change of mission, I knew combat cargo pilots would face a whole new peril. We'd all heard about flying the hump, and we could do the math. Our planes normally flew at below 22,000 feet, and the peaks in the Himalayas are much higher than that. Even before we got to Myitkyina, I saw a whole new challenge ahead. The mountains in the region were much higher than our planes' altitude capability. We would have to fly through the mountain passes at times, rather than over the mountains. This was a problem in stormy weather when zero visibility obscured the mountains in our flight path.

"The peaks themselves thus prevented us from flying around the storms. Monsoon storms were violent and deadly."

25

Dead Reckoning

The FAA defines Dead Reckoning as the process of estimating a global position by advancing a known position, using direction, speed, time, and distance of travel. Before modern radio technology and electronic navigation, pilots had to figure out where they would be at a certain time if they held the speed, time and course of their current flight pattern. Sometimes these calculations proved accurate; other times not. Without aids during inclement weather, these combat cargo pilots lived with constant uncertainty about their calculations—Dead Reckoning was all they had. They never knew the conditions or the direction of the winds that would blow them off their plotted course.

Max explains Dead Reckoning this way: "Today, pilots have sophisticated instruments to let them know where they are, where they're going, and what's ahead. But when we were flying over there, we would look at the map and say, 'We're flying from point A to point B. Our destination is, say, thirty-seven degrees from where we are.' Then we would just fly thirty-seven degrees on the compass. However, that didn't take into consideration the wind direction and velocity, which were unknown."

Before a mission, Max would study his route. "Say we were in Burma, and I was planning to fly into China. I would study the map and, based on my own previous flights and the testimonies of other pilots, I would draw a flight chart. I had to precisely nail where the mountain passes were, because obviously I couldn't fly over mountains that were higher than the airplane's altitude capability.

"So my crew and I would take off, with the plane groaning under the burden of weight, and for a certain number of minutes we'd fly in a particular direction at a certain airspeed and rate of climb. After a calculated number of minutes, we had to take a new reading and ascend at a constant rate of climb, maintain a steady airspeed, check our direction, and try to avoid hitting the mountains. And at the same time we changed course, we had to gain altitude.

"Inclement weather meant we could never rely on visuals, which is why we had an instrument traffic pattern and specific routes to fly, and it was dangerous to deviate from that pattern. Our instruments were basic, including the airspeed indicator, altimeter, compass plus directional gyroscope, and a rate of climb indicator. Even so, on sunny days, it wasn't so hard to fly these routes visually. In India, Roger King, the British locator unit, had helped us pinpoint our location. Over the hump, though, we were on our own. We had no aids at all.

"We put forth our very best effort to work out all the conditions ahead of time, using the information we had, often from other pilot reports, and to draw a good flight plan. Even so, there were always unknown factors that could render our flight plan moot. Once we got into the air, we might find that the wind direction was not what we expected, or that a violent rain storm had thrown us off course. If a storm was in our flight path, we usually had to fly straight through it, as mountains were on all sides of us. So we had no choice but to rely on our flight chart during inclement weather, but we also called on our experience and instincts, because there was always inclement weather, and inclement weather required continual navigational skills. If our visibility was zero, or if we hit an unknown fierce wind, we could be moved sideways instantly. That's when it would be so easy to slam into the side of the mountain.

"Apparently I was fortunate and used correct judgment at the proper times, because I'm here, years later, talking about these events."

On clear days, on the approach into Kunming, Max would see dozens of charred, deeply indented blemishes in the mountainsides, where pilots just like him, trying to land during monsoon weather, had died fiery deaths. "I knew some of those guys, but I didn't mentally dwell on it when I was flying," he says. "I stayed as focused as possible. I tried to put aside every distraction. I thought only about what I needed to do next."

26

Scenes of War

As they occurred, and for years afterward, the scenes of war had a hallucinatory quality for Max and his fellow combat cargo pilots, as again and again they descended into the line of fire. He remembers these missions now in a dreamlike way, but also with clarity. Even now, fifty years later, he has nightmares about those scenes. He thrashes around in bed. He's not conscious of this during his waking hours, but there are scenes of war that continue to haunt him:

"I remember coming in for a landing at Myitkyina Field, along with a number of other pilots trying to land during a dense monsoon fog. In those circumstances, planes would stack up as they attempted to make an instrument landing in hazardous conditions. We were all coming back from missions in China, and we had crossed the Burma Boundary and were over the Burma Valley before we could get radio contact with our home base in Myitkyina, where we wanted to land.

"During the monsoon season, fog sometimes settled into the Burma valley from ground zero up to as high as 30,000 feet. This made instrument landings necessary, because we had absolutely no visibility. But we were all having difficulty pulling off instrument landings in these circumstances. Even without the zero visibility, there was the hazard of dodging other planes in this fog.

"Planes were stacking up as we got ready to come in for a landing. We were assigned a holding pattern of 22,000 feet, and a hold on the vertical radio beacon at the airfield. Planes were stacked every five hundred feet below us. When the bottom plane would make a landing, the one above it would descend five hundred feet, and the one above that one would descend five hundred feet, and so it would go, layer by layer, until everybody had a chance to attempt a landing.

"The problem was, we were all coming back across the mountains from a long flight, and we didn't have a full tank of gas. Since we had to wait our turn to land, and each landing took several minutes, lots of guys ran out of gas and had to bail out. It was night, and of course we couldn't see through that thick fog or the darkness. I located a searchlight that I knew was positioned at the end of the runway, and it was boring through that fog. I made my first circuit on that searchlight. I just put my left wing on the beacon and descended from there. Riding a search light was a crude way to make a landing, but it worked better in those circumstances than the radio landing.

"Throughout that night, people radioed to say they were running out of gas, that they would fly for certain minutes longer, and then bail out. I remember there were guys walking back into the field for a week after that, trying to get back to base from wherever they had landed. Of course some of them never did make it back."

27

Leaving the China-Burma-India Theatre

One day the war finally ended. Max recalls, "When the war was over, we were instructed to come home according to the decorations that we had received, added to points we could accumulate by virtue of other factors, such as how many children we had, and so forth. I was in Myitkyina, Burma, at the time, and we were instructed to catch a ship out of Karachi, India, hundreds and hundreds of miles away. Our orders were to take a narrow-gauge train across Burma, and then across India, all the way to Karachi. The trip would take about ten days." Max and his cohorts found this completely unacceptable.

"Well, we'd been in intense combat, and it didn't seem palatable to us to take a damn train for more than a week to get to Karachi. We didn't much like the ATC (Air Transport Command) guys who flew supplies in to us, because they wouldn't fly if the weather was bad. So a bunch of us decided that we would help ourselves to one of their airplanes.

"Their field was about twenty miles from where we were located. Hugh King and I had somebody take us over to their airfield at 2:00 in the morning. When we got there, we boarded one of their C-46 airplanes, which were identical to our planes, and we flew it back to base to pick up twenty or so other guys. They loaded their barracks bags into the cargo hold and we started for Karachi.

"On the way, we landed at Dum-Dum Airport in Calcutta to

refuel our stolen airplane. All we did was take the gasoline truck and refuel our plane. Our safety measures were not too tight, obviously, as I still have a picture of one of the pilots standing on the wing of that stolen C-46, smoking a cigarette as he put gas into the plane.

"We flew all the way to Karachi, parked the airplane at the Karachi airport, grabbed our barracks bags, and left the plane sitting on the tarmac there.

"Later we met a couple of pilots who were going to China, and we told them where the plane was located, but I have no idea whether they picked it up.

"All I know is, we were out of there, and within thirty-six hours, we were on the way home."

Open cockpit PT19 pilot Max Carr, Stamford Field, 1944.

Proud mother, Mary Carr, with newly Commissioned Officer Pilot Max Carr, in front of the family home on Roscoe Avenue in Akron.

Outside Cairo, Egypt, en route to combat in the China-Burma-India Theatre. Max is in the center.

"Flying the Hump" (Himalaya Mountains) required an oxygen mask.

Unloading supplies and ammunition for Ghurka fighters in Burma.

One of Max's favorite co-pilots in China was Hugh King, pictured here.

Ghurka fighters such as these were among the most decorated soldiers in World War II.

Basha boys helped care for U.S. and British soldiers. Here, they are pictured in front of the basha. Max's favorite, Abdullah, is third from the left.

Above:
Home at last. The
Statue of Liberty is
viewed from Max's
"liberty ship."

Max remained in the
Reserves after the war.

These are some of the medals Max earned for his WWII service.

Left to right, top, row 1:
1. 10th Air Force patch
2. 14th Squadron—You Call It We'll Haul It—4th Combat Cargo Group
3. CBI patch—China-Burma-India theatre

Row 2:
1. Distinguished Flying Cross
2. Wings: (a) USAAF pilot wings; (b) Chinese Air Force pilot wings, presented by General Lin Wenli, Commander in Chief, Chinese Air Force, Republic of China; (c) U.S. Army aviator
3. Air Medal with 3 oak leaf clusters: 4 total awards of medal for 283 combat missions

Row 3:
1. American Campaign
2. Bronze Star
3. Asiatic Pacific Campaign with 3 battle stars: India-Burma, Central Burma, China Defensive (U.S. Army designated campaigns).

Row 4:
1. World War II Victory
2. U.S. Army Good Conduct
3. National Defense with bronza star: duty during 1950-'54, and during 1961-'74
4. Armed Forces Reserve, U.S. Air Force branch

Row 5:
1. Burma Star, awarded by the government of Great Britain for providing aid to British Army forces fighting the Japanese in Burma
2. Army Air Corps officers' collar wings
3. Army Air Corps officers' cap badge in gilt
4. China War Memorial Medal, awarded by the government of Republic of China for providing aid to Chinese forces fighting the Japanese
5. Lieutenant Colonel collar insignia rank
6. Ribbon Bar: Distinguished Flying Cross, Bronza Star, Air Medal with 3 bronze oak leaf clusters, U.S. Army Good Conduct, Army Reserve Components Achievement Medal, American Campaign 1941-1945, Asiatic-Pacific Campaign with 3 battle stars, World War II Victory, National Defense Medal with bronza star, U.S. Air Force Longevity Service with silver oak leaf cluster (for 20+ years service), U.S. Armed Forces Reserve.

Max, when he retired as a Lieutenant Colonel

PART THREE

HOME FROM WAR

28

Homecoming

At war's end, soldiers, sailors, airmen, and other military personnel were sent back to the United States on Liberty Ships. Max joined hundreds of others on one of these ships leaving Karachi for New York.

"We were crammed on board as we left India, but I have happy memories of that passage. I remember a former child movie star named Jackie Coogan was aboard ship. He'd been a glider pilot in the China-Burma-India Theatre, and he really made a hit with the nurses on the ship. People were very optimistic, and happy to be heading home."

Even nature seemed to celebrate with the returning soldiers, who saw whales and dolphins and various other marine life along the way. As an added benefit, because ocean travel was not speedy, the journey provided the men with time to begin the transition back to the life they had known before the war.

An unexpected highlight of the trip for Max was his first taste of milk in months. Of course there had been no milk among their K-rations, and when he tasted its delicate sweetness he realized how much he had missed it. Like his fellow pilots, Max had eaten very little while he was in the C-B-I Theatre— that is, until the last dozen or so weeks, when a fellow named Major Cox, who was the father of one of Max's fellow pilots, started making flights to Calcutta and returning with meat and a dense, dark bread. But milk? "Nothing ever tasted better," he says.

Since he'd left home, Max's weight had dropped from 165 to 130 pounds.

From the Red Sea, the Liberty Ship passed through the Indian Ocean, through the Gulf of Aden to the Red Sea, through the Suez Canal to the Mediterranean, past the Rock of Gibraltar, into the open waters of the Atlantic Ocean, and finally homeward.

"When we had been traveling in open waters for about three days, and all we could see in any direction were water and sky, we came upon a Liberty Ship much like ours that had broken apart," Max recalls. "It had just split in half, leaving no sign that we could see of survivors. This sobered all of us. Those guys had been so close to home, with the worst supposedly behind them! It seemed like a bad omen, and we had to work to shake it off."

Days later the ship propelled into New York harbor to ringing bells, tooting whistles, and cheers. "People were holding homemade signs reading 'Welcome home' and 'Victory,'" Max recalls. "I saw a huge message constructed of whitewashed boulders on the hillside ahead. It spelled out, WELL DONE. I was moved and impressed.

"We disembarked and went to a processing center in New Jersey, where the authorities collected all our data. The paperwork took a couple of days, but when it was done, we found ourselves separated from military service, just that easily. The military provided railroad transport to the chosen destination of each returning soldier, and I picked Austin, of course. I needed to get back to my wife and children."

In time, Max boarded a train that, like the Liberty Ship, was crowded with other men like himself, men who had seen too much, fought plenty, and developed the hardness necessary for survival. Maybe they were ready to shed a little of that hardness now. Max certainly was. "I'd had enough of war," he says. "I wanted peace and quiet."

It was at the railroad station in downtown Austin that he first saw Mae Belle.

"I was stepping off the train when I caught sight of her and her older sister, Ruth, waiting off to one side. I had been away for months. I had changed, and I hadn't known Mae Belle very well to start with, so I guess I could have expected my homecoming to be a little awkward. But I have to admit that I also expected a warm welcome.

"As soon as I spotted her, I rushed over to hug Mae Belle—and she pushed me away, saying she didn't want a public display of emotion. I looked around. All the other returning soldiers were being hugged, but Mae Belle kept shooing me away, saying, 'Later!'

"It hit me then that she and I really were strangers—and yet we had a child together."

Max followed Mae Belle and Ruth to the car and the three of them drove to the Rice family house at 1507 Lorraine in Tarrytown, where Mae Belle and the children had been living while Max was overseas. Max remembers pulling up in front of the familiar house:

"By the time we got there, it was evening. When I walked inside, I saw my daughter Kathy for the first time. She was just an infant, but she was already bright-eyed and alert. I also saw again this beautiful little boy, David, that I had inherited when I married Mae Belle.

"I felt welcomed by the family. As the evening wore on, it became obvious to me that everyone had agreed ahead of time not to ask questions about what I'd been through. They were trying to be sensitive, and I appreciated it. Instead, we talked about the family, the children, Dixie's business, and what had gone on at home during the months I'd been away. We were trying to get reacquainted."

Because of the intensity of combat, Max had rarely written letters from overseas. However, Harris Philquist, who was married to Mae Belle's sister, Ruth, had filled the family in about Max's assignment in the China-Burma-India Theatre. Harris' authority in the matter came from two or three times Max and he had managed to get together in Burma. When he returned home, Harris told the family he didn't see how Max would ever get out alive.

The Rice family at that time included parents Marie and Dixie, their five children, three sons-in-law, and six grandchildren. Louise was the oldest child in the family, and she was married to Jack Starkey, Max's friend from Bergstrom Field. Next in line was Ruth, married to Harris Philquist. Mae Belle followed Ruth. When Max rejoined the family, Mae Belle's younger sister, Florence, was a teenager, and Tom, the baby of the family, was approaching his teenage years. Including Mae Belle, David, and baby Kathy, seven people were living in the family house when Max made it eight, taking his place beside his wife in the big upstairs room, an open, loft-like space that included five people in four beds. Jack and Louise and their two children lived in an adjacent garage apartment. It was a crowded house, with various uncles, cousins and other relatives living at the house from time to time. "Needless to say, there was no privacy," Max says.

As he went about those first days back, he tried to forget all about the war—and he found that was easier said than done. He felt jumpy and guarded. In fact, he gradually began to recognize how thoroughly he had compartmentalized his emotions while he was overseas. "I had worked hard to control my emotions when I was flying combat missions," he says. "I couldn't afford to be distracted by fear."

Now home, though, he remained revved-up, as if to fight, and at the same time he was occasionally blind-sided by an odd post-war paralysis. One afternoon a few days after his return, for example, he was driving down the street when he passed a grocery store. He wanted some chewing gum, so he pulled up in front of the store and parked the car. "But I couldn't make myself go inside," he recalls. "I didn't want the gum enough to walk in there and talk to people. I didn't want to talk to anybody.

"We didn't have a name back then for what's now called Post-Traumatic Stress Disorder, but I must have had something akin to that," he says. He didn't want to think or talk about the war, but holding it in required so much nervous energy that even jogging through his days at work and working on construction projects at night didn't expend it all.

"Even worse, I wasn't sleeping well. I had nightmares, and I'd wake up feeling threatened and disoriented, sometimes flailing my arms. These dreams went on for years. They go on today. You'd think this would stop."

Soon after his return, Max knew he needed to get back to

Ohio. After all, he was still on leave of absence from the phone company there, and Max was a man who took his job obligations seriously. That work equals success had served as a motto for him since his early teens. Work equals success. Never take a job for granted.

He broke the news of their move to Mae Belle, who objected strenuously. She didn't want to leave her family. She'd always lived in Austin, and she never wanted to live anywhere else.

Further complicating matters was the fact that Marie Rice was very attached to David, so she, too, protested the idea of Max's moving the family. "David was such an endearing child," Max says, "and my mother-in-law hated the thought of not having him near."

Despite the family's objections, though, Max and Mae Belle and the children did leave for Akron. It was winter 1946, and it was freezing cold in Ohio. "Since Marie Rice was originally from Ohio," Max says, "there were plenty of relatives around Akron, both from Mae Belle's side of the family and from mine. That came in handy for us, because there was a terrific housing shortage after the war, and Mae Belle's uncle had a little two-bedroom cottage that he made available to us."

As the family settled into its new home, Max began work as a residential installer for Ohio Bell. "I was starting at the bottom with the company," he says, "but I'd expected that. After the war, the hard truth about working for the telephone company, or any other large corporation, I guess, was that if you had a college degree you were on an automatic career path. You had to make a real effort before you could mess up your promotion schedule.

"But if, like me, you didn't have a degree, you had to earn recognition through measurable results and unusual talents. I had to work harder to distinguish myself. Luckily I'd always had a competitive nature. A psychologist would probably trace it back to my childhood poverty, but for whatever reason I always measured myself in comparison with others. I wanted to make the most calls, the fastest, and the most efficiently. I always wanted to win. From the day I returned from the war, I understood what I had to do if I wanted to advance. I had to out-do the guys with the college degrees."

To that end, Max installed phones and phone lines throughout the cold Ohio winter. When the mercury reached twenty below zero, he just worked faster. He was often out in isolated rural areas climbing ice-crusted poles. "I made a point of installing more phones per day than anybody else in the work force," he says. "I clocked myself."

One day when he was working, he had a bit of a surprise. Jogging up to the front door of a house on Lucy Street, he suddenly realized he was at the family house of his classmate, Alberta Poukas. He supposed Alberta would be long gone from home by now, but as he rang the doorbell, he couldn't help reflecting on how she'd been the object of his desire for so many years. He remembered the clumsy note he had passed to her in the movies on that long-ago Saturday. He thought of how, when he was a boy staring at the kits then available in the Sears & Roebuck catalog, the ones for assemble-it-yourself small homes and cottages, he would dream of growing up to live in a house like that, and it was always Alberta beside him in these fantasies.

His thoughts were interrupted when the door was opened by Alberta herself. "Max?" she said, surprised. "Is that you?"

They talked, and naturally she asked about his war experiences. He told her only a few bare facts, and changed the subject. He was on the clock so he couldn't stay long, but he didn't miss the irony of that experience. "Here, only a few years after high school, was the woman of my dreams, the lovely, black-haired girl I'd fantasized having a life with. She was not married, and when she asked if I was, I said no. I just couldn't tell her that I was married and a father. I tried, but I couldn't. 'Maybe we ought to get together,' she said. But I never did call her. By this time, we had each established our path."

Max continued to throw himself into his work that winter, but as grey days became grey weeks and then grey months, he found himself dreaming about the sunshine and mild winters in Texas.

Mae Belle, meanwhile, was desperate to move back to Austin. "She was just lost in Akron," Max says. "She was so close to her family. They'd done everything together throughout her life. She and her mother had talked every day, always. Mae Belle just pined for her family."

In Akron, of course, Max's family was nearby. Okey and Mary liked Mae Belle and the children, but they never fussed over them. "My parents were matter-of-fact people," Max explains. "They were not the sort to spoil or coddle the kids. So they couldn't fill the gap that Mae Belle felt in being away from her family. Besides, my dad was a common working man, and he and my mother had neither the money nor the opportunity, and probably not the desire, to social climb in any way. It must have been hard for Mae Belle to adjust to the hillbilly class of people that I came from."

As the weeks passed, Max gradually decided that he would ask for a transfer to the phone company in Austin. "For many reasons, moving back to Austin seemed wise," he says. "For one thing, in Akron we were living in the house of a relative, which had to be a temporary situation. As I said, there was no housing for returning vets, in Texas or Ohio or anywhere else, but I had been assured by Mae Belle's family that if I would bring the family back to Texas, Dixie would help us find housing."

Max liked Austin, and not just the weather. It was a friendly town, and he knew people there. He could imagine rising in the telephone company in Austin. And it would be nice to be near the Rice family again. "I got along well with Dixie and my brothers-in-law," says Max. "So all the signs were pointing toward a return to Texas."

AT&T was the parent company of all the 'baby bells' at that time, including Ohio Bell and Southwestern Bell, so transfers within the industry were possible. "When I asked for the transfer, though, Ohio Bell tried to get me to stay. 'You have a future with Ohio Bell,' the manager told me. But my mind was made up. We were moving back to Texas. What I was looking for at that point was serenity, and living in Austin seemed my best shot at it."

However, Southwestern Bell had no openings, nor could they foresee any.

Max was undeterred. He requested a ninety-day leave of absence from Ohio Bell, and when it began, he immediately moved the family back to Austin, and back into the upstairs loft of the Rice family home.

Now what? He was on leave from the phone company, he was living at his in-laws', and for once in his life, he wasn't on anybody's schedule—so what did he do? "I immediately started working with my father-in-law and his partners building houses," he says. "I couldn't imagine just sitting around. I was geared to work, but I'll tell you, that was hard work. Dixie asked me to go into business with him and Jack and Harris, and I thought about it. But the truth is, I didn't like that work. I didn't like dealing with sub-contractors, or having so much of the process out of my control.

"I missed the phone company."

In a stroke of good timing, two days before his leave of absence was to expire—at which point his choices would be to move back to Ohio, or quit the phone company—Max was contacted by Southwestern Bell that there was a job for him. As in Akron, he was hired as a residential telephone installer. It was a craftsman's job, and Max knew that he would be starting at the bottom, once again proving himself.

He was ready.

29

Max's New Job

"I hit the ground running from my first day on the job at Southwestern Bell," Max recalls. "I was so glad to be back in Austin and, as I had been in Akron, determined to be better than anybody else at completing job assignments. I never did lose that competitive feeling. As I rose through the ranks, I just raised my goals. I made sure I excelled in every measurement."

Life at home, though, was not so straightforward. Through his experiences in the military and in the workplace, Max had developed a strong attraction to the logic of action and consequence. He'd come to believe, in other words, that if one gives a problem his best effort, good results will follow. "I always said to myself that I was smart enough to solve any problem. I still believed that, if I just thought a problem through, just tried hard enough, I could come up with a solution. But as I was trying to assimilate into my life in Austin, I was having a hard time making things work at home."

Time helped a little. As weeks and then months passed, Max began to feel enough distance from the war that, as he puts it, "My nerves began to settle down. Only the nightmares remained and I figured I was going to have to learn to live with those."

Of course the fact that they were living with the Rices didn't make it easier for the young family to establish itself, so Max turned his energies to finding a place of their own. He had accumulated about $12,000 in poker winnings during his time in the military, and he decided to use that money to build a house.

Step one was to buy a lot.

Max's new lot was at the corner of Cherry Lane and Dillman Street, in the heart of Tarrytown. The area was still sparsely developed in 1946, and the Carrs' corner was crammed full of cedar trees. "I cut them all down myself," Max says. "I'd go over there every day. Usually I worked alone, but I was glad for a hand if a brother-in-law or friend happened to offer one.

"My first task was to clear enough trees to allow me to pour a foundation. I knew it was not going to get any easier to buy a house in this growing city, and I needed to get my family out of the Rices' house. So I became driven about working on the house every spare minute.

"I drew my own house plans—and they were later utilized to build other houses in the neighborhood. You can drive down Clearview Street and see several houses built on the plan I drew, including one I helped A.C. Warner build for himself and his family."

Even after he started his new job with Southwestern Bell, Max continued to work on the Cherry Lane house every night. Not satisfied with working during the long hours of daylight, he hooked up some lights (though unauthorized to do so), and with that he was able to continue working after dark. He routinely worked sixteen-hour days.

"I just managed to buy all the lumber and materials with my poker winnings," he says. "The lot itself had cost about $1,500, so I had a budget of approximately $10,500 for materials and supplies. I decided that when I got a little more money set aside, I would finish out the upper level. But I wasn't going to wait until that happened to move my family.

"In 1947, there was a sixty-day strike at the phone company. I took this opportunity to complete the first floor and frame in the second floor. Then I moved the family in."

It's a good thing Max decided not to put off moving until he had finished the entire project, because it was another five years before the house was complete. When finished, the house was two stories, four bedrooms, with a one-car attached garage. "As it happened, it took as much money to finish the second floor as it had to build the whole lower level," he says. "That was my first hard lesson in inflation."

But inflation didn't stop there. Because he built the house with his own sweat, Max invested a total of only about $25,000 in that house over the fifteen years the family lived there. Sixty years later, in 2007, the house—very little changed—was sold for $750,000.

30

Homelife

Now that the family was settled, and now that he was established with the phone company, Max felt his old calm gradually returning, and as it did, he realized he missed flying. "At some point, I realized that if I joined the Air Force Reserves, I could fly," he says. "The Air Force was created in 1947, after the war, so it was brand new in those years. It was now an entity separate from the Army Air Corps, which was what I'd been in as a combat cargo pilot.

"Another benefit of joining the Reserves was that I would be paid a little. I began flying out of Bergstrom, and flying became one of my favorite emotional outlets. I was gone one weekend a month, flying. My favorite thing was to fly the Kaiser T-28, a high-powered single-engine mono-plane, out of Brooks Field in San Antonio."

In 1952, Max was asked by Southwestern Bell to set up a training school for phone company employees. "I was a good student, always interested in electricity, and I had a pretty deep knowledge of the theories and equipment used in the telephone industry," he says. "Consequently, when they needed an instructor to teach new employees about innovations in the phone industry, I was asked to be an instructor in the first training school ever opened by Southwestern Bell. The school was in San Antonio, so I drove a ninety-mile round trip back and forth for a year. I finally got tired of the drive and moved the family to San Antonio. For a year or so, we lived on Rayburn Drive, and enrolled the kids in school. Our house was just a few miles from

Brooks Air Force Base, which made it easier for me to fly those T-28s on a regular basis.

"Sometimes there'd be a gap in the schedule at the phone company school, and when I had no classes, I'd head over to Brooks, snag a plane, and do some flying. In Reserves, we had to fly a certain number of hours per month in order to maintain flight status. During one of these private flying episodes, I'd picked up a T-28 and I was flying around Austin when I got a call from the tower at Brooks telling me that I had an emergency at work. So I raced back to Brooks at full power, landed, and called Slim Howell, my fellow teacher. He said I should get over there quick.

"The Division Plant Superintendent and some other officers had come by the school to see me, and Slim, trying to cover for me, had told them I'd been called home because my wife was sick. So when I arrived, they were waiting for me, and they asked after Mae Belle's health.

"'Oh, she's fine,' I said. 'She's out working in the yard.'

"At this, Slim looked stricken. But either the managers didn't notice that he had been caught in a lie, or they were pretty broad-minded. In any case, they weren't there to chew me out, but to tell me that I was being promoted to a higher level management position. As a teacher, I was in a first-level management job, and I was being promoted to a second-level management job. I would now supervise all Austin telephone equipment installers. It was a big responsibility, but I felt prepared.

"A few days earlier, Slim had bet me a $50 Stetson that I'd get promoted back to Austin within a short time. I took him up on the bet, and this promotion meant that I had to buy him the hat. As soon as I gave it to him, though, he admitted that he'd been informed of my promotion ahead of time. That rascal had known he was betting on a sure thing. Oh, well, I liked ol' Slim. He taught me to play Dominos, and we often gambled during our lunch hours. Just small bets."

Max and the family moved back to Austin then, and back

into their house on Cherry Lane. Mae Belle and the kids were glad to be back, but there wasn't much joy in the house. Max describes these years of his marriage as "dry and matter-of-fact. Mae Belle was a beautiful woman. She looked a lot like Lauren Bacall. But her expression and demeanor were very sad. She always expected bad things to happen. And nothing you could do or say would persuade her otherwise.

"Mae Belle ran an orderly house. She was a good cook, and an excellent mother. The house was always nice. It seemed to me that our family functioned pretty much as most families at that time did, so I tried to be satisfied. I figured that if I just kept doing the right thing, eventually she would come around."

31

Growing Up
on Cherry Lane

Kathleen Marie Carr
David Thomas Carr

"Dad and I were very close when I was growing up and in school," remembers his daughter, Kathy, now retired from thirty-two years working for the City of Austin. Her final job there was as assistant manager of customer service for Water and Wastewater. "We'd play cards, games like Crazy 8. I still like to play cards. Dad taught me to love games.

"We used to ride together in the same car, and there was one spot on Enfield Road where there was an island, and every time we'd get to that place Dad would say, 'Get the big picture, Kathleen. Get the big picture.' What he meant was, 'Think about the traffic, think ahead, and get into the right lane so you can turn.' In other words, he was telling me to think ahead about what I was doing." As it turns out, this was more than metaphor with Max. "He always tried to help me make better choices," she says with a laugh. "No doubt it was good advice."

Max says, "Kathy was a fun-loving girl. She liked to have a good time. She was upbeat."

"I think I learned my love of people from my father," Kathy says. "Daddy was very charismatic. He drew people to him. He asked about the other person, and he listened when they talked about what they were doing."

The family was socially active. Of course, the Rice family was the center of their social life, but even beyond the family, as the neighborhood grew up around the house on Cherry Lane, Max and Mae Belle often had company.

Kathy appreciated her mother's skills around the house. "My mother was an immaculate housekeeper. She made all my clothes, even my underwear. She made my canopy bedspread. She would starch Dad's shirts and then press them just perfectly."

Remembering their family life, Kathy goes on, "I don't ever remember seeing my folks drink, unless company came over or something. Mother and Dad had about six couples that they ran around with. When I was growing up, people used to play bridge, and those couples would come over for games and supper. We used to play croquet, too. We always had a croquet set in the back yard.

"Family Friday nights would entail going to the drive-in theatre. Mother would give David and me a bath and put us in our pajamas before we went to the movie. That used to embarrass me. On Sundays we'd just drive around town for entertainment."

Max was often gone, working long hours at the phone company, slaving away on a building project, or logging flight hours. But even when he was home, he stayed busy. "Dad wasn't one to sit around. He would make things, or work at his work bench," Kathy recalls. "He didn't fish, but he liked to make sinkers. He had a little Plaster of Paris mold, and he'd pour melted lead into it, and when it cooled it would be a sinker. He had buckets of those."

David remembers how precise Max was about his tools. "One thing that sticks in my mind is that Max was always very careful with his tools. If something was hanging up in a particular place, that's where it needed to be returned. He was strict about my putting things back where I found them."

The reason Max needed his tools handy is that he always had a project going. When he finally completed building the house, and helping A.C. Warner with his, he started on a boat. David remembers it well. "It was an old cabin cruiser that slept two people, with a bed on either side," he says. "I think Dad must have replaced every screw in it. He completely rebuilt it, and worked on it for years. He sanded it down and everything. He kept it on the side of the house."

The road was still unpaved when the Carrs moved to Cherry Lane, and there were no curbs or sidewalks then. "It was very natural," Kathy said. "I remember dozens of big horny toads throughout our back yard. Once Dad and I were at the side of the house when we saw a huge tarantula over by the two cedar trees next to my parents' bedroom window. Dad told me that tarantula was going to jump on me. Scared me to death. Even today I'm terrified of large spiders."

Max was always puttering outside. "Dad could grow anything," Kathy recalls. "He would take an oleander branch and cut it just so, and put the parts in coffee cans where they would root, and then he would plant them. He always had rows and rows of oleander cuttings out back, just waiting to root and be planted. The oleanders he gave our neighbors across the street are still thriving today."

David says, "Max didn't like yard work much, though, as I recall."

"That's for sure," Kathy agrees. "Remember Willie Kocurek? He used to live catty-corner across from us and his yard was always immaculate. Oh, Mr. Kocurek had a beautiful yard, flowers blooming, everything mowed and trimmed. There was so much color in his yard. And of course, Dad disliked yard work, so ours was never well-kept.

"Well, one day Mr. Kocurek came over and asked Dad, 'So, Max, what are your plans for your yard?' This became a real joke in our family. What were Dad's plans for our yard?" She laughs.

Lyndon B. Johnson and his family lived two houses north of the Carrs in those days. "The Johnsons used to have parties outside, with lights strung in the trees, and caterers in white coats walking around serving the guests," Kathy says. "Also, Jake Pickle lived about three blocks away."

The Carr children remember their childhood as similar to that of their friends, including one ritual familiar to anyone who grew up in the Sixties. "Remember those big machines that sprayed DDT to kill the bugs?" Kathy says. "We kids in the neighborhood would want to be outside following it, and Mother and Dad would holler at us to come inside. Good thing they did. That was poison, but we didn't know it then."

Kathy remembers how much fun her dad was whenever he was home. "He walked on his hands like nobody else," she says. "He once walked on his hands all the way around the block."

Max built a sturdy picnic table in the back yard on Cherry Lane. "It was made of poured concrete and rocks, and it looked indestructible," Kathy says. The family sometimes ate supper out there, and Kathy remembers those evenings. "Daddy used to walk around shirtless, and one day we were sitting out at the picnic table when a little neighbor girl walked up and said, 'Mr. Carr, who took all that hair off your head and glued it on your chest?'"

The years passed, and the children grew into teenagers. David started high school, and Kathy moved into junior high. "There was a tree, an oak tree, and it grew up beside the house and curved up to the flat roof by my bedroom," Kathy remembers. "At slumber parties, my girlfriends and I used to shimmy down that tree in our baby doll pajamas and then we would head down the street to toilet paper a friend's or boyfriend's house,. We didn't think anything about it. Nobody would ever be out at that hour.

"We did this so many times that Dad accused us of stunting the growth of that tree."

When Kathy was about fourteen years old, she and Max went to Niagara Falls to see Ford and Ethel. "I don't remember why David and Mother didn't go," Kathy says, "but it was only Dad and I on the trip. We played mind games the whole way. One of us would say, 'I'm thinking of something. Can you guess it?' It was amazing how, sitting together in the car, we could each figure out what the other was thinking.

"We had a lot of laughs on that trip. We'd notice things and get completely tickled. For example, on this pig farm in Virginia, in an area where the people were really backward, we saw this little girl with two pigtails coming out the side of her head and one from the top. We laughed about that for weeks.

"After we left my Uncle Ford's, we went to visit Dad's parents. My grandparents here in Austin had the attitude that their grandkids could do no wrong. They spoiled us. But it wasn't like that with Dad's parents; in fact, I was scared to death of his father. They lived out on a farm in a tiny house without running water. The well was outside the door, and my grandmother would have to get the water and put it on the stove to cook with. There were wash buckets and chicken pens. They also had an outhouse. Dad's father told me that that was all quicksand out there, and that if I walked too far out, I would sink. That was to keep me from wandering around.

"My grandfather had an old tractor that we'd crank up and drive, and he'd let us ride through the apple orchard. But he always warned us not to waste the apples. Of course, I had to do what he told me not to, so one day I went along picking up apples one at a time, taking one bite of each, and then throwing it on the ground. The next day my grandfather gathered up all those apples and confronted me with them. I got quite a chewing out!

"One time, don't ask me why, I decided to play a joke on my grandfather. I lay on the kitchen floor and covered myself with ketchup. Then I got a knife and made it look like I'd been cut. He didn't think that was funny. He cut a branch off a peach tree and trimmed it off for a switch, and he started chasing me up the dirt road. I kept hollering that I didn't like the granddaddy in Ohio because my granddaddy in Austin wouldn't do me that way.

"Dad's father was quite a character, though. He was from another era. I remember he played Solitaire so much that he wore his cards all the way through. You could see where his thumbs went on those cards. They were completely worn through from his shuffling.

"As for Dad's mother, I remember she spoke with a strong northern accent. And I remember what a hard worker she was. She always had an apron on. She'd be working in the kitchen, always pumping that water, always at the stove. She had a basement just lined with shelves and shelves of food that she had canned and put up: peaches, peas, beans, okra.

"I don't remember her ever sitting down."

32

The Lake House

While it was true that Max didn't want to go into the construction business as a profession, it was equally true that he had a gift for designing, engineering, drawing up plans for, and building structures. This was satisfying work to him, a nice supplement to his job at the telephone company. So when he finished building his own house; finished helping Mae Belle's Uncle A.C. Warner with his, on the next block; finished lending a hand with an additional couple of houses on Clearview Street that were using the plans he'd drawn for his own house—at that point, Max needed another project.

The year was 1957. "I was working for the phone company, and I wasn't making much money," says Max. "I liked my job, and I continued to excel by every available measurement. But I wanted to be equally productive during my non-working hours.

"I guess I had a lot to prove."

Max had always dreamed of having a house on the lake, and when a friend of his from the phone company, George Potoff, invited Max out to his fishing cabin on Lake Travis, that desire blossomed. "You got to Potoff's place by way of a little two-lane dirt road," he recalls. "There was nothing out there. It was completely undeveloped.

"Well, I did some research and found out that a man named Rucker owned the land adjacent to George's lake place. It was a beautiful lot, situated right at the curve of the Colorado River, completely natural. The view extended for miles both up-river and down-river, and the property also bent back into a private cove. It was 450 feet of lake frontage, all in one large parcel. Boy, I wanted that property.

"I called Mr. Rucker and asked his price: $1,800. That was completely out of my range. So I went to A.C. Warner to see if he wanted to go in with me. He did, and the two of us called Mr. Rucker and said we would meet his price. We were just voices on the telephone to him, but we came to an agreement during that conversation. He agreed to sell the whole parcel to us the following Friday.

"George Potoff, who was now my next-door neighbor every weekend, later told me that another buyer had called Mr. Rucker right after A.C. and I did, and had offered him twice our price. But Mr. Rucker refused, because he had given his word."

Immediately after signing the papers, Max began drawing a plan for a house on a prominent point overlooking the river. On the opposite bank was a point of land with one stately rock house at its tip. Otherwise, for as far as Max could see, no buildings were in evidence.

The two partners jumped right in to the project. Max was twenty years younger than A.C., and in terrific physical condition, so he did most of the manual labor. "The first thing I did was to draw a crude house plan. Then we poured a twenty-feet by forty-feet concrete slab on the place," he says. "On one end of the slab, we put in a women's bath and a men's bath, which together measured six by twenty. That was a good start."

However, just as they finished out the bathrooms, A.C. Warner's contracting business went bankrupt. "This was less than a year after we bought the land," Max says. "A.C. offered to buy me out, or to let me buy him out. On my salary, I knew I'd never have another chance to own a place on the lake. So I told him I'd buy him out.

"And I didn't have a cent."

Ever resourceful, Max came up with a plan for completing the transaction. "I divided the land in half and sold the back half of the property for the amount of money I needed to pay off everything A.C. and I owed on it. As a result, I actually ended up with 250 feet of lakefront property that didn't cost me anything. I sold the part on the cove for what we'd originally paid for the whole, which meant I owned my part free and clear."

So Max had the land, but he had no money for supplies or materials to build a house. "I decided just to use what I had," he says. "I would go up there with a pick and a bar, and I'd pry up rocks to use in the house. There's a layer of stone on this property, and I'd hack out rocks with that pick, some of them weighing three hundred pounds. Then I'd take a sledge hammer to break up the larger pieces. I was going to build a rock house anyway, so I figured I might as well use the rocks that were on the place. It was a labor intensive process, though, and it made me glad for the experience I'd gotten as a stone mason back in Akron, during that brief period that I worked for the WPA.

"Every weekend I'd bring a sack of cement to the lake and start from scratch. I built a wooden box to mix the cement in, and then I started building the walls one rock at a time, with only my original crude drawing to go by. The reason I hadn't been more detailed about the plan is that I knew the house was going to evolve over time.

"But my original idea was to build a one-story house with rock walls. So I picked up lumber wherever I could find it, and used discarded telephone company cross-arms for studding.

"Inside the house, I left a number of insulators in place to add a little character."

It took maybe two years for Max, usually working alone, to get the house framed in. He headed out to the lake every weekend, as well as many nights, to pour concrete, put up studs, and build roof rafters. The house gradually took shape until, in a couple of years, it was weathered in.

Max's kids have clear memories of the years when their dad was building the lake house. "He was constantly working on that house," Kathy says, "and he was doing it all without spending money. Dad never wasted anything; he reused everything. For years he would pick up old nails and straighten them up and reuse them. And he would use boards he found lying around, as well as discarded lumber from the telephone company. Every rock he used to build the house was picked up off the land there."

David says he wasn't much help on the Lake House, but as the years passed, he became very interested in it. "At first when Dad was building that house, I helped some, but not a whole lot. I didn't have a whole lot of interest in it," he says. "The truth is, Dad built the entire thing himself. He went out there every weekend, and he just made progress little by little. I remember how he mixed the concrete in a wheelbarrow or in his handmade wooden box on the ground. He mixed it with a hoe. That's the hard way.

"As the years passed, I kind of caught the bug, too. I started picking up a piece of lumber here or a big rock there, and incorporating it into the design. Sometimes I'd go to the lake on a Friday night and sleep out on the roof of the building and just work during the day. That house just kept evolving, for years."

Max agrees. "I continued spending time at the lake. It was the only form of recreation I had. There were times, much later, when I was able to hire a few things done—but in those early years, I did the heavy lifting myself. It was impossible for me to pay for labor or supplies."

By 1960, the lake house was a low, one-story hut, flat-roofed, and rock solid. "Sometimes after a flood, lumber would wash up on the shore and I'd pick it up and use it," Max says. "And Kathy's right, I didn't buy nails, either. I scrounged them out of old lumber. It was fun because when I found something, I could use my imagination as to how we could use that in the house. I can look at almost every rock and tell you where I got it."

It was always clear that the house was an evolutionary project and, for the next forty years, Max never stopped working on it.

33

Becoming a Painter

Max is a talented painter, mainly a portraitist, and in this as in so many areas, he is self-taught. It all started with one encounter. "I've mentioned that there are different levels of management in the phone company," he says. "Well, as I made my way up the ladder, I worked for all different managerial types. Some of them were decent fellows, but others had big heads. In particular, I remember one district plant superintendent who rotated through Austin. While he was here, I reported to him. I always tried to have my office neat and orderly, in hopes my subordinates would see it and conclude that that was the way to do things.

"So I liked my office, but I thought it looked bare. I asked this supervisor for an oil painting to warm up my office, and he haughtily replied that second-level managers like me didn't rate a painting. Such frivolity was against company policy, he claimed. So I thought, *Well, you bastard, I'll just paint my own.*

"I didn't have a canvas, but I had an old cabinet, so I tore the back off and used the flat surface to paint on. I didn't have paint, but my friend Paul Parker gave me some dried-up tubes and small cans of paint. I didn't have brushes, but the kids had brushes. So I just took what I had and made a painting, the first painting that I ever tried.

"That supervisor was later demoted to a lower level of management," he adds wickedly.

"As for me, the experience made me realize I really liked

painting. It was relaxing to me, and also a way to focus my mind. When I'm painting, all my creative energies are on that canvas.

"From that first painting, I have gravitated to painting with better paints and brushes. I've never had lessons. Years later, I did a painting of four children in the Andes, and I was offered a million dollars for that one. Can you believe it? By then, though, I didn't need the money, and besides, the painting in question was like one of my children to me. Very precious.

"I always liked western themes. After a while, I thought, *Well, maybe I'll try to paint a cowboy or two*. I still didn't have canvases, so I used plywood. I painted a gambler, and a barroom girl. These were copies, from memory, of some paintings I had seen and liked.

"I want to correct something I said. I did try, once, to take painting lessons. I went to a class for three days, and on the third day the teacher was showing me how to do a certain technique and she smeared paint all over my painting. I left and never went back.

"A few years later, a professor from the University of Texas looked at some of my paintings and he said, 'Don't go to art school, Max. It would ruin you. Just paint what you feel.'

"That turned out to be good advice, because as much as I enjoy painting, it's not something I want to be analytical about. It's one activity I'd prefer to do by instinct. So every two or three years, when I get an urge, I complete a few paintings. I don't have any real knowledge about it. I couldn't begin to tell you how to mix colors. And I don't go to museums.

"I just like to paint."

34

Braided Lives

David Thomas Carr,
Max's son

"I didn't find out that Max wasn't my biological father until I was eighteen or nineteen years old. To tell the truth, I don't remember exactly when it was, but I know we were still living on Cherry Lane. It seems like somebody told me, and I remember I got real mad. I guess I've blocked out exactly what happened, but I do remember that it bothered me that everybody in the family except for me knew Max wasn't my real father. My theory is that if you're adopted you ought to know about it. It shouldn't hit you like a ton of bricks.

"As soon as I got over the shock of finding out that Max wasn't my birth father, I didn't feel any different about him. He was still the only father I've ever known. I call him Max or Dad, whatever. He has been a strong positive influence throughout my life. People say I inherited my work ethic from him.

"I guess this is odd, but Max and I never once discussed the fact that he wasn't my biological father. I think the underlying feeling between us was that he was my father in every way except for biological. We were both committed to that basic fact."

Tom Rice,
Max's former brother-in-law

I was approaching my teens when Max and my sister Mae Belle got married, and then immediately he was gone to war.

"So it wasn't until Max came back that I got to know him a little better. What I learned was that he has a fierce sense of right and wrong. He's basically a non-aggressive person, but you don't step on his toes. He won't tolerate someone hurting someone he loves. He's protective of the people he is close to.

"I also saw how he likes to putter. He was always working on something. We'd go up to his land on the lake and fish for carp, not the best eating fish in the world. I remember one day Max and I decided we were going to grill some carp. There's an old joke that if you're going to cut a carp on a cutting board, you should throw the fish away and eat the board. Well, that day, we caught a carp and tried to grill it. Not only did we throw the cutting board away, but we also threw the grill away!

"Another time I went up to his lake place, and as I approached I smelled fire. I rounded a corner and saw that Max was clearing some cedar off the property, and he'd started a bonfire with the wood. As I watched, he stuck a fork in a piece of meat and extended it into the fire, cooking it on the spot. That's the caveman in him!"

Kathleen Marie Carr Hobbs, Max's daughter

"One thing people don't know about my dad is that he knows how to yodel. He's actually pretty good at it.

"He has a lot of sides. He's not a big cook, but everybody in the family remembers his cheese soup. For every holiday and every other time we all got together, he would make that soup. Everybody loves it.

"Hey, I have the recipe, although I think I'm the only female in the family who has never actually made it. Here it is:"

CANADIAN CHEESE SOUP

¼ c. butter	1 qt. whole milk
½ c. finely diced onion	at room temperature
½ c. finely diced carrots	⅛ tsp. soda
½ c. finely diced celery	1 lb. processed cheese

¼ c. flour	salt & pepper
1½ T. cornstarch	2 T. finely chopped parsley
1 qt. chicken stock	
at room temperature	

Melt butter in the soup pot. Add onions, carrots, celery—and sauté over low heat until soft. Add flour and cornstarch, and cook until bubbly. Add stock and milk and make a smooth sauce. Add soda and the cheese, grated. Season with salt and pepper. Add parsley just before serving. (Be careful. Don't let the soup boil.) Serves 8

Dennis Harris
Fellow phone company employee and long-time friend

"Max Carr has had a more profound positive impact on my life than anyone other than my parents, because he's a model of strength, wisdom, and integrity.

"Thirty-nine years ago, the Amarillo Air Force Base was closed, and I was the supervising installation manager for Southwestern Bell there. The base closing meant I had surplus employees that I didn't have enough work for. Someone suggested I call Max Carr, who had the same job in Austin that I had in Amarillo. With the University of Texas rush, he might need help at that time of year. I called Max, and we became instant friends on the phone even though I'd never talked to him before. He said, 'I can take all you can send me.' So I loaned him eighteen installers.

"About a month later, I was transferred to Victoria, Texas, and Max was the first person I called. It wasn't long before Max had arranged for me to join his National Guard group in Austin, a very elite selective service unit. Whereas in the past I'd always dreaded my monthly National Guard obligation, I now started looking forward to it, because I knew I would see Max.

"It didn't take long after meeting him to figure out that Max was the go-to guy for any group he was associated with. People asked his advice because he was experienced, smart, and not arrogant. He was the best at how to build relationships and deal with people with different points of view who were having problems. He knew how to motivate organizations, how to treat people with respect, and how to get the most out of people.

"In those days, there were many combative relationships in dealing with the union. Many, many managers never learned how to deal with people and get good results. But the union had so much respect for Max that he could get more out of them than anybody could.

"I had monthly district meetings at which my subordinate managers would assemble to talk about the business. One year I asked Max to come and speak to this large group about how to manage people, and how to work with the union. I wanted him to share his philosophy with the group.

"In response to my request, Max gave the issue of his managerial philosophy considerable thought. Then he put together this incredible speech—eloquent, clear, riveting. In fact, it was more than a speech. It was a blueprint for success in dealing with people. He was a big hit at the conference. His remarks were timeless. His ideas spread through the crowd, with everyone talking about it, and everyone demanding a copy of the text.

"A few years later, Max had moved to another organizational level in the phone company, so we were no longer in the same structure. I was in the Houston area and he was in San Antonio. With a new audience, I again asked him to come and give that speech, so he came to Beaumont and spoke to my people there. Again his speech was so successful that his listeners requested the text. For years, Max's speech functioned as a *de facto* guide to management for the phone company, one that was passed hand-to-hand, from old employee to new.

"Here's the thing. Max always saw things more clearly than other people did. He had the ability to analyze problems and find solutions that other people struggled with. In his business dealings, he played it straight, took the high road, and didn't panic.

"He always said it was easy to run the business part of the equation. It was the people part that took skill and patience."

35

Rising in the Phone Company
1946-1970

Max continued through the levels at the phone company, from his start as a residential telephone installer through supervisory levels, and from working as a craftsman to managing employees throughout a vast territory. Eventually he became a plant superintendent for Central Texas. For most of those years, he was headquartered in Austin, though various assignments took him elsewhere for brief periods.

Interestingly, though, some of Max's most memorable experiences during his years with the phone company could be described as tangential to his work. Max hopes the Statute of Limitations has expired on at least one experience. He explains, "In the early 1960s, a fellow named Dub Naylor was head of the Department of Public Safety Narcotics Division. I met him through A.C. Warner, who was a friend of his. Naylor's group wanted to do some wiretapping in their narcotics operation in Texas and he came to me to figure out the technical part. The problem was, wire-tapping was illegal. Even so, I became an integral part of that operation. I thought it was necessary to stop this kind of crime.

"At one point, a U.T. boy killed two girls in his apartment and hid them in a closet. and then had a party that night. The partygoers were unaware of what was going on. The authorities had a suspicion that this person was the assailant, but they couldn't prove it, so they made arrangements for me to move

176

into an apartment adjacent to the suspect. I was to try, through wiretapping or any other means, to obtain evidence against this guy. I really was an unpaid member of that narcotics group.

"However, on the day that we started the operation, the guy walked into the police headquarters and confessed.

"Also through Dub Naylor, I met Ann Desoto, a beautiful young blonde prostitute only nineteen or twenty years of age. She was married to this Mexican fellow who headed up a drug trafficking ring, and her husband had fled to Mexico to avoid prosecution. Dub Naylor had decided to offer him amnesty if he would testify about the entire operation. So Dub and I drove to Nuevo Laredo to meet the head of the drug ring in Pappagallo's House of Prostitution and Bar, an old dancehall. Dub and his agents were dressed like drug dealers so that they would blend in. Dub had dyed his hair green, and he had a way-out look about him. He looked like riff-raff. I, too, tried to dress so that I would be inconspicuous.

"Desoto made his appearance and sat at the table with us while we drank whiskey sours and watched the prostitutes circulating through the room. Pappagallo's was actually kind of elegant. It reminded me of Miss Kitty's place in 'Gunsmoke,' with its dance floor, band, alcoves with beaded curtains. Prostitutes would sit around in all stages of undress.

"Well, that evening Dub and I were sitting there with Desoto when two other law enforcement people from the U.S. showed up. One was a detective from Houston, and the other was a member of the border patrol. All were dressed in civilian clothes and looking disreputable.

"Later, another of Dub's young agents, a good-looking guy in his mid-twenties, came in with a beautiful blonde prostitute from the U.S. Dub had teamed his officers up with prostitutes so that they could live in the criminal world. He explained to me that he would not accept a young agent in this dirty business unless, if the young officer was married, he first talked to the man's wife and explained what kind of world her husband was getting in to.

"So this young guy appeared, and he was high on drugs. The other law officers were kidding him. His face would twitch, he would smile and laugh. I thought, *Boy, Dub is right. This IS a nasty business*.

"All through the night we were trying to get Desoto to rat on his fellows, but he wouldn't do it because he was afraid he would be killed."

Over time, Max acquired a reputation for being knowledgeable about telecommunications and also willing to help the law. Byron Hildebrand was one of Max's friends. He worked in the commercial department of the phone company, and he was responsible for taking orders and collecting payments.

"One day Hildebrand told me, 'I'm liable to get fired because I can't collect this enormous amount of money from one of the customers.'

"Being curious, I asked, 'Well, who is it?'

"'I can't tell you. Confidential. But it's a young lady who lives on a circle in South Austin. She's making a lot of calls to a hotel in Mexico City.'

"I asked, 'Is it Ann St. Augustine?'

"Of all the customers in Austin, I had picked out the right name. This was Ann Desoto's maiden name. She was calling her husband, handling drug business by phone.

"Hildebrand was astonished. 'How did you know?' he asked.

"Of course I couldn't tell him how I had guessed. But I did say, 'I think I can get your money for you.'

"I happened to know Ann was sleeping with a prominent local contractor/developer. So I called Dub Naylor and told him that Ann Desoto had a big telephone bill. I said it almost had to be in connection with the drug ring. I told Dub to call the contractor and tell him that Ann Desoto had been identified as participating in drug trafficking, and that if Byron wasn't paid, he was going to see her sent to the pen. So the contractor paid the bill.

"Meanwhile, Dub traced the numbers she had been calling, and through that information, they identified and broke up that drug ring."

Piloting had gotten into Max's blood during the war, so he was happy when the United States Air Force was formed, as separate from the Army Air Corps. In 1950, he joined the active reserves, which gave him two clear benefits: it paid a supplemental income, and it allowed Max to fly in the reserve contingents at Bergstrom Air Force Base. "I continued with that pretty much through the 1950s," Max says. "But then I became curious about helicopters. I had never flown helicopters and I found out I could do so in the Army National Guard. So I switched back to the army and started flying helicopters out of Camp Mabry. That took quite a time commitment, but in time I became commander of the helicopter company. I continued this until I got the civilian assignment to oversee the communication requirements of President Lyndon B. Johnson, both in Austin and at his LBJ Ranch.

When I realized I wouldn't have time to keep my pilot qualifications up, I talked to General Bishop about getting off flight status. The general agreed, adding that he had wanted to place me on his staff.

"Early the next morning, I got a call from a reporter saying, 'How do you feel about being commander of the first reserve helicopter company to be activated for service in Viet Nam?' I said I was surprised at this news. I hadn't heard anything about it. So I called the General and he said that it was a fact that, eight hours after we had talked, the helicopter company had been activated.

"The general explained that he had named me Deputy Director of Selective Service. This was a responsible position, but not a flying position. I saw it as a way for me to keep my hand in the reserves and still have the time to do this important task of providing President Johnson's communication needs. So I accepted the general's offer. In January 1964, I ended my military flying career."

36

Providing Presidential Communications

After Lyndon Johnson was sworn in as president following the assassination of John F. Kennedy, Southwestern Bell was notified that LBJ would require a communications system at his ranch equivalent to that in the White House. This would be a massive project—and it had to be completed in two weeks!

Due to his broad experience and understanding of communication requirements, Max was made coordinator of the project. "At the time I was a second-level supervisor," he says. "Because I had declined to leave Austin, I was only two levels above being a craftsman. This was a decision I had made. I didn't want the hassle of upper management, and even though I was asked several times to take management positions, for example in St. Louis, I didn't want to move. Part of this was family. Part of it was that I just wanted peace and quiet. Sure, I was ambitious in wanting better things for my family, and I always wanted to do my best—but I didn't want the headaches of higher level management. Despite my management level, though, I had the technical knowledge to provide the president with the massive services he would require."

Max recalls that a member of the White House staff named Joe Taylor was sent to Austin to take the fall when, as was widely expected, the president's communication needs in Johnson City and Austin were not met by the time the President and his family would be in Texas for the Christmas holidays.

180

"We'd been given what was considered by many to be a futile task," Max recalls. "In two weeks we were to build microwave routes, cable routes, and to have installed a massive amount of telephone equipment. We had to equal what was installed in Washington, D.C., and we had to do it from scratch in a bare field in only fourteen days. People were positive it couldn't be done. In fact, I had executive-level people warn me not to be destroyed by the fact that we probably couldn't provide what the president was asking for. The more people warned me, though, the more I wanted to rise to the challenge."

Hundreds of phone company employees were assigned to the project. Max says, "I received the assignment on a Friday, and I immediately went out to survey the ranch. There was an oat field next to LBJ's ranch house. By Monday, just two days later, we had erected a 90' x 120' building, using pre-hardening concrete and sheet metal. This would be our center of operation, and we managed to complete the entire structure over that first weekend.

"Next we had to install phone equipment for microwave transmission circuitry to D.C., drawing cable routes from Austin, San Antonio, and Johnson City, and then installing underground cable any place around Johnson City that the president might visit. During the course of this project, there were times when a vice-president of another company in the Bell System would call, and I would have to dictate what was required and how it was going to operate.

"One part of our assignment was to replicate the White House switchboards in a trailer next to the president's ranch house. There were eight 608 PBX's, where the operators manually handled incoming calls and directed outgoing calls. There were actually operators working twenty-four hours a day, seven days a week whenever LBJ was in Texas."

Max recalls some of the Secret Service guys who worked with him in Johnson City. "I had met this fellow named Rufus Youngblood before Johnson became president. When LBJ was Vice-President, Rufus would come with him to Austin to check on the communication lines. In fact, he was the man riding on the rear bumper of the car when Kennedy was assassinated."

Max remembers the Secret Service agent in charge, a man named Clarence Kinish, as well as many others involved in the project.

But he especially remembers Joe Hunt. "Joe Hunt was Vice-President of Operations in Texas for Southwestern Bell," Max says. "He's the one who appointed me to this position. He asked around to see who was most qualified, and my name came up."

Joe would call Max at midnight, and Max would tell Joe what he needed—people with specific qualifications, or particular equipment. "Then Joe would show up at eight the next morning, bringing whatever was needed. His ability to provide what we needed made the whole operation possible.

"As we were working on it, sometimes I wouldn't sleep for two days at a time. We would have two hundred people working in this building, installing termination equipment for local circuits being established all over the Hill Country.

"When the president came back to the ranch for the Christmas holidays, just weeks after Kennedy's assassination, he landed in Air Force One in San Antonio and headed for the ranch in a smaller jet. We had been working like madmen for two weeks, and now I told the crew to power up the system. And as soon as we applied power to all of our equipment, bells started ringing, red lights started flashing, and everything was signifying massive failure. One of the workmen, Foxworth, cried, 'I'm sorry! I did it!' And really he had caused the failure. He had short-circuited a circuit he was working on, and a transient voltage had entered the multiplex, which was the nerve center of the operation. Within minutes, though, we looked at the multiplex, made a quick determination about how to remedy the problem, switched the operation to a good power supply, and everything worked. We never had a failure after that, for the entire time LBJ was in office.

"As a result of our success, Joe Taylor became a golden boy in the military. He always credited me with saving his career."

As to his impressions of LBJ, Max says, "He was one of the strongest-willed people I ever met. He was smart. I would describe him as devious, except that he had enough power that he didn't have to be devious—he could be just outright tough. I know that he was tough on his subordinates. One day when I was at the ranch, I saw this General walk out the kitchen door of the ranch house. He walked over by the trailer where I happened to be, and he sat down and put his head in his hands. I was shocked to see that he had tears in his eyes. I don't know what kind of verbal beating he'd gotten, but that man was suffering.

"Johnson was one of the most adept politicians ever, though. Straightforward, very strong. He knew how to get what he wanted from people. He was the most capable politician I ever saw or knew of.

"Of course, Lady Bird was in evidence on all the television pickups. She struck me as one of the kindest and most considerate people on the face of the earth. And she had to be tolerant to put up with her husband."

LBJ came to Max and Harold Stienke, who worked for Max in the Austin Southwestern Bell office, and asked how he could have a conversation on the phone without anybody's eavesdropping on him. "He was visibly upset," recalls Max. "We didn't know how it might have taken place, but apparently he thought that somebody had eavesdropped on a phone conversation. We told him that we had taken every precaution in the world to ensure that his communications were as secret as they could be. We told him that, electronically, there was just no way, at his location, that we could assure one hundred percent protection. The only way we knew of to have a completely confidential conversation would be for him to take the person out to the end of his runway and whisper. Within a week of this conversation, the President made the surprise announcement that he wasn't going to run again."

37

A New Face
in the Company

In the late 1960s, Southwestern Bell had a program for recruiting promising recent college graduates into the company. The hope was that these young people would energize the company and also make a long-term commitment to Southwestern Bell.

"These new people were coming into the organization in management positions, which was unusual," Max explains. "They didn't come up through the ranks. Naturally, there was resentment among rank and file employees who aspired to promotions into management when they saw these newcomers cut in line that way."

Meanwhile, there was plenty of publicity for the program. In-house newsletters were full of profiles of the new employees, including one young woman who had graduated from Vanderbilt University.

"I'd read the stories," Max said. "This Cassandra Colvin had been a beauty queen and I could see why, from her photographs. She was brunette, with an open, friendly face. She was accomplished and she had million-dollar looks. I figured she was probably so full of herself she'd be insufferable. I had no interest in meeting her."

At the time, Max was Supervising Installation Foreman. He was in charge, in other words, of installation of residence and business telephone service, and the many employees who provided it. His territory covered a widespread area of Central Texas.

A supervisor in the traffic division, Dan McRae, brought Cassandra to meet Max because Cassandra, as a management employee in the traffic department, had her first assignment, which required the cooperation of Max's division. Cassandra was ambitious; she wanted to do well right off the bat, and for that to happen, she needed Max's support.

"I was responsible for supervision of plant department activities, which included the employees who worked in subscribers' homes. Dan and Cassandra, meanwhile, worked in the traffic department, which handled the calls that were made to the switchboards and the central offices. Our two divisions were separate, but worked together very closely.

"My office was in that building, but because I had come up through the ranks, I never wanted to separate myself from employees who were lower down in the organization. I liked to relate to everybody, so I had no qualms about turning a waste paper basket upside down and sitting on it, if there wasn't a chair nearby.

"I was sitting on an upended trash can talking to a woman at her desk when I saw Dan and this young lady approaching. Like everybody, I knew who the woman was. I'd been reading about her, and hearing about her through the grapevine. A few days earlier she had been on an elevator with this guy and when he got off, I happened to be walking by. He said, 'I have just met Miss America.' He was completely dazzled.

"So here they came, walking toward me: Dan and this vision of beauty. She was wearing orange tights that disappeared up under a tiny purple mini-skirt. I said to myself, *I, for one, am not going to fall at her feet*, and when Dan introduced us, I kept my seat on the upturned trash can. Very graciously, Cassandra extended her hand. After we shook, the two of them explained how the traffic department needed to inform subscribers of direct distance dialing. They wanted my installers to hand out brochures and answer questions through face-to-face contact when they went into homes to do installations."

Max heard them out, but he reserved judgment—both about their request and about Cassandra Colvin herself.

He didn't know it at the time, but his life had just taken a dramatic turn.

Max built the family home at 3207 Cherry Lane in Austin himself, using winnings from his poker games during the war.

In the back yard of his Cherry Lane house, Max build a picnic table to last.

Max as a young father, with Kathy and David.

David and Kathy loved to drive their Grandfather Okey's tractor when they visited Ohio.

Clockwise from top left:

Kathleen Marie Carr as a high school student

David Thomas Carr as a high school student.

Max Carr's official Southwestern Bell photo.

This is Max's first painting, which he painted on the back of a cabinet door.

Cassandra took a photo of these children, who were standing alongside the train tracks between Machu Picchu and Cuzco. Max then painted it and was offered a million dollars from a potential buyer. He declined to sell it.

Max painted this one for his mother, when she was bedridden.

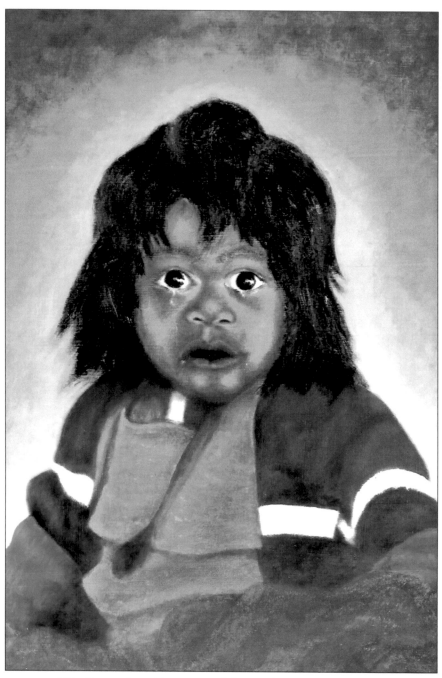

This Guatemalan girl was painted from a photo taken by a friend.

PART FOUR

A NEW LEASE
ON LIFE

38

Cassandra

Cassandra Colvin grew up, mainly in Kentucky, the older of two daughters of a Baptist minister, Rev. A. B. Colvin, and his wife, Irene Shearer Colvin. Rev. Colvin was known as "Mr. Kentucky Baptist" for his wide-ranging influence in that denomination. Cassandra occasionally felt as though her father's job was somehow hers, too. "My sister and I had to stay in line," she recalls. "I always felt I needed to be perfect."

Cassandra went to Vanderbilt and graduated with a major in English. She pledged Delta Delta Delta and, when she was twenty years old and a junior, competed in the Miss Louisville contest, winning the title of Miss Louisville, Kentucky—1965.

After graduating from college, Cassandra decided to move to Dallas and look for a job. "I chose Texas," she says, "because I had never met anyone from there who didn't like it. I figured if Texans liked living there so much, it must be the place to be." She wasn't sure what she wanted to do, so she explored the job market while doing freelance modeling at the fairly new Apparel Mart, and working as a temp for various companies. For one two-week period, she was a secretary. "I had to bring the boss coffee," she says. "Obviously I didn't last long at that."

About six months after moving to Dallas, Cassandra heard about the Management Training Program at Southwestern Bell. The company was hiring recent college graduates, putting them through rigorous training programs, and then integrating these talented young people into the company. It sounded like a fit, and Cassandra signed on. Her first title with the company was

Group Chief Operator. As such, she supervised a group of long-distance operators.

After half a year, in the first of what would turn out to be many work-related moves, the phone company transferred Cassandra to Austin. In January 1967, she married Joe, a young man she'd known at Vanderbilt who was then a student at the University of Texas School of Law. That marriage ended exactly two years later, in January 1969.

Meanwhile, Cassandra continued her work at the telephone company, broadening her experience in every way she could, so when the company was ready to introduce Direct Distance Dialing (DDD) a year later, Cassandra was chosen to be a part of the initiative.

"She asked me to have my installers explain to the customer, at the time of installation, the advantages of direct distance dialing," Max says with a chuckle. "Planning how to do this necessitated many conferences between Cassandra and me. Sometimes we met in my office, other times in a conference room. At first I kept it strictly business, and held myself back emotionally. However, it didn't take long for me to realize that I had misjudged Cassandra."

Cassandra remembers those meetings as professionally critical. "My future success with the company depended upon my getting Max's cooperation," she says. "I had to persuade him to allow his installers the time to explain the program. My boss had told me that Max was revered in management, and in fact by everybody in the company, because of the way he did his job. But he also said Max was sometimes a tough nut to crack, because he wouldn't do anything unless he could see that it would help his team's results. And here I was, asking him to do something that would actually hurt his team's results, because his installers would have to take the time to explain DDD, which in turn would make them less efficient.

"So I was uptight about meeting him. After my boss and I outlined the program to Max, he didn't agree right then and there. It wasn't until a few days later that he agreed to try it, just to see how it went. In fact, I don't remember a point when he said, 'Yes, I'll do what you need me to do.' He just agreed to see how his guys responded. He didn't make it easy for me at the beginning."

Max recalls, "During those meetings, I found Cassandra gracious and highly intelligent, but also unassuming. This surprised me. How could anybody so beautiful be so unaware of it? There was nothing put-on or phony about her."

Meanwhile, "I was not aware that he was finding me attractive," Cassandra says. "That wasn't on my agenda at all. I just knew I had to have his cooperation. I was coming into the company at first-level management, and since I wanted to be as successful as I could, I was task-focused. I was taking one step at a time because I wanted to move up to second level. That was as high as I could see. At that time, no woman had ever been past second-level management."

Max says, "Gradually, our conversations became more personal. Cassandra was separated and in the process of divorcing, and Mae Belle had recently moved out. As Cassandra and I talked, we learned things about each other, and a friendship developed."

It turned out the public loved Direct Distance Dialing from the very beginning, and the DDD program was a rousing success. "Cassandra and I had a dinner date one night, to celebrate our success," Max said. "This led to more dinner dates, and before long, we realized we had deep feelings for each other."

As the weeks went by, although Max and Cassandra didn't make a show of their relationship, people at the company caught on. "Even though we were both executives, there was no problem at work," Max recalls. "People were happy for us, and supportive."

Max and Mae Belle were divorced in late 1969. "Anybody who has ever been through the dissolution of a marriage, with all its emotional attachments, knows that it's a hard thing to do," Max says, in reflecting on those events. "I've never said a bad word about Mae Belle. I have a lot of respect for her, but we were incompatible. It's really as simple as that.

"However, things turned out well for everyone. Mae Belle married a fine gentleman, and from all reports, they enjoyed a rewarding life together. It was a good marriage. She and her husband, Jack, traveled together, and she got to see more of the world. Jack was a graduate of U.T. and an enthusiastic supporter of college athletics, so he took Mae Belle to all the games. I was happy that they found each other and that, at long last, life for Mae Belle was happy."

The relationship between Max and Cassandra deepened further as they spent 1970 exploring their relationship without any plans for the future.

Max swears Cassandra was the one who finally made the proposal. "One night she said, 'You know, Max, if we don't get married, we probably won't be together a year from now,' and I thought, *What a devastating idea*! I was horrified at the thought of not having her in my life."

So Max and Cassandra decided to get married. "At that time, a marriage license in Texas cost $5.00, and Max and I split the fee fifty-fifty," says Cassandra with a chuckle. "As you can see, we were on an equal footing from the beginning."

Then they began the requisite two-week wait until they could make it official.

"On the afternoon of the fifteenth day," says Max, "the Friday after Thanksgiving, we went to San Marcos and we were married by a Justice of the Peace. Then we drove to Nuevo Laredo for a honeymoon."

The newlyweds stayed at the El Rio Motel. "That was a beautiful hotel, in my opinion," says Max. "It had adobe buildings, and courtyards with roses, semi-tropical flowers, palm trees, and swimming pools. Located about three miles south of Nuevo Laredo, it was Mexico at its most beautiful."

While at the hotel, Max and Cassandra enjoyed meals in the hotel dining room. "It was very fine," Cassandra remembers, "with indoor fountains and pressed white linens, and with Mexican paintings on the walls."

In El Rio's dining room, the two met and befriended a young waiter named Ismael Rodriquez. Out of that meeting a whole new adventure grew, setting a pattern that would persist throughout the years of their marriage. Whether by decision or instinct, Max and Cassandra are open to people who might escape other people's attention. This hallmark of their marriage perhaps began with Ismael, the first of many people whose acquaintance would lead to adventures in unexpected new places.

"Ismael was a waiter, but he was also the president of some of the unions in Nuevo Laredo," says Max, "so he occupied a prominent position among the working people in town. As he waited on us and learned that we were newly-weds, we all became fast friends. He was very personable. At age thirty-two, Ismael was always looking for the next big thing. He told us stories about 'thees opportunity,' speaking of the development taking place along the Rio Grande at the time. Hotels were going up in Nuevo Laredo, he said. Restaurants were opening. He was so enthusiastic it was contagious. Before our honeymoon was over, we knew he hoped to open a restaurant/bar in Nuevo Laredo. This was his dream.

"As I have said before, when I squandered the chance to buy that big ruby during the war, I made up my mind never to miss another opportunity. Maybe that's why, when Ismael mentioned his idea, Cassandra and I decided to put a few thousand dollars in a bank account for him as start-up money. From time to time, while the enterprise was still in the planning stages, Ismael would come to Austin. He'd just show up at our house in the evenings, and he would always have a new opportunity to talk about."

As it turned out, the Carrs' honeymoon was memorable for reasons beyond their meeting Ismael. "The first couple of days we were in Nuevo Laredo," says Max, "we enjoyed the night life in the city. Then on Friday night, I figured we had covered the scene in Nuevo Laredo, so I said to Cassandra, 'Well, what are we going to do tonight?' And then, being a smart-ass, I joked, 'Let's go to Pappagallo's. It's over in Boys' Town.'" Boys' Town is the red-light section of Nuevo Laredo, on the Mexican side of the border.

"I had no intention of really going there, but after I made the suggestion, Cassandra insisted that she wanted to see this. So we drove to Pappagallo's, and we could almost have found our way by following the dust rising on the road, because so many cars were heading that direction."

"We were driving that 1965 white Chevy," Cassandra adds.

Max nods and goes on, "Boys' Town is surrounded by an adobe wall, probably twelve feet high, and armed guards are at the entrance. Usually the guards let visitors right in, but when Cassandra and I tried to enter, they stopped us."

"In order for me to enter the place, Max had to give them $25 for a license," Cassandra says. "That was the rule. I had to be licensed as a prostitute, or I couldn't go in."

Max takes up the story. "So we got her licensed and entered the bar where the dance floor was and sat down at the table. Cassandra's eyes were as big as saucers. The little preacher's daughter had never seen anything like this. There were fifty or sixty girls in all stages of dress and undress, sitting or walking around the room.

"We ordered drinks—whisky sours—and I intentionally gave the waiter twice the amount he asked for, thinking that if we got into any kind of trouble, he might see fit to help us out of there. Remember, this is the same place that I had gone years earlier with the narcotics officer. I knew things could get rough fast.

"I looked over at Cassandra, and I noticed that she was holding her hands in front of her eyes, looking out through her fingers. I told her to take her hands down, and try to look normal for the surroundings. After about three whisky sours, she was sitting on my lap, blowing in my ear.

"A while later, she suddenly tensed up. 'What's wrong?' I asked, and she said that one of the men in the booths was motioning her over."

For the next couple of hours, Max and Cassandra just sat at a table nursing drinks, taking in the sights, and talking in low voices. "Now this is funny," Max remembers. "We were making conversation when Cassandra mentioned that, according to office scuttlebutt, a fellow at the telephone company in Austin (who, incidentally, was in love with her), was supposed to be in Nuevo Laredo that same night. I said, 'Wouldn't it be funny if we saw him in Pappagallo's?' and just then, so help me God, I looked up and he was not ten feet away, walking towards our table. He didn't know we'd just gotten married, and in any case, he didn't see us. He walked within a foot of my chair.

"As he passed, I called his name. He hesitated, probably thinking, 'Nobody knows me here,' so he walked on. I called his name again, this time first *and* last names, and he turned around and approached me, his hand extended. Just then, he saw Cassandra and realized that we were together. He just turned on his heel and walked away. What a shock this must have been for him. I felt sorry for him.

"Later on, after Cassandra got back to work, she was telling some friends at the office that she had run into their co-worker in a Mexican whorehouse. They were laughing uproariously when someone suddenly thought to ask, 'But Cassandra, what were *you* doing in a Mexican whorehouse?' She replied, 'Oh, I was on my honeymoon. And by the way, I became a licensed prostitute while I was there!'"

"When we left Pappagallo's, I made Max take me out through the back door like all the other girls," Cassandra concludes, laughing. "I didn't want to leave through the front door and have people think I couldn't get a customer!"

39

Inside an Alaska Prison

From the beginning, adventure was a big part of Max and Cassandra's marriage, and in 1971, a spontaneous decision led them to some surprising new acquaintances—and to several near-misses in terms of their personal safety. Max explains. "We hadn't been married long. I had always wanted to go to Alaska, so Cassandra and I decided to plan a trip there. In preparation, we bought an El Camino pick-up truck, which we would use for the driving part of the trip. I put a top over the bed of the truck, which provided an enclosed space for sleeping. Next we bought tickets for boat passage from the western port of Prince Rupert, Canada, on the inland coastal canal. We were all set for an Alaskan adventure."

Then, in a perfect example of bad timing, the phone company went on strike. "Of course, since both Cassandra and I were in management, we were obligated to work during the strike," Max says. "We worried that we were going to lose all the money we'd paid for the trip, as well as the experience we'd planned, but it turned out that the strike ended within three or four days of our original departure time. 'Hey,' I said to Cassandra, 'if we drive 900 miles a day, we can still catch that boat.'

"So we put a half mattress in the back, grabbed a Coleman stove and lantern, and a 32-calibre rifle—and we were ready to camp out. We planned to sleep in the truck bed as we traveled around Alaska. We headed north, with me as the driver and Cassandra as the navigator. Her job was to determine how far we had to go each day in order to reach our destination—the boat in Prince Rupert—in time.

"We drove like hell and covered 830 miles a day. At night, we would heat something on our stove for supper, and then crawl back into the bed of the truck and close up for the night. As we slept, I kept that 32-calibre rifle pointing toward the tailgate, in case somebody wanted to cause a problem.

"The night before we were to catch the boat at Prince Rupert, we pulled in to a remote spot along the highway, high in mountainous territory. Exhausted but relieved, we were only two hundred miles from Prince Rupert. It would be no problem to make it the next day.

"I was dead-tired, and after eating a little something, I was ready to sleep. We crawled into the enclosed truck bed and collapsed. As we talked about how we were going to catch the boat the next day, I was tired and out of sorts. It occurred to me that we needed to check the tickets and trip paperwork, so I asked Cassandra if she'd go up into the cab and double-check our departure time. Being a good sport, she agreed to do that, and when she came back she was laughing.

"'What's so funny?' I asked in a grumpy voice.

"'I just checked the tickets,' she said. 'We don't have to be in Prince Rupert until two days from now.'

"My navigator had miscalculated, and it was easy to see that my insane driving schedule could have been more sensible.

"So we arrived early to catch the boat. We put the truck in the hold of the ship and had a stateroom for our quarters. The boat left Prince Rupert and went up the inland waterway. We stopped at two or three places along on the way, and we'd get off the boat at various towns. This is a trip that I'd advise anybody to take: the wilderness, birds, animal life, and sea life are spectacular—and also there's an opportunity to see various Indian cultures along the waterway.

"Our destination was Haines, Alaska, a town about which I had been curious since it was struck by a huge tidal wave a few years earlier. I remembered seeing a documentary about national disasters that included this event. In the film, a man happened to be standing on the deck of a freighter ship with a hand-held camera when an earthquake took place, followed minutes later by a huge tidal wave that hit the Alaska coast. He took a movie in which he panned the town, and his film included this one unforgettable shot of a little boy pulling a wagon, with a little spotted dog running alongside him. As that huge wall of water came ashore, it just swept the little boy and his dog away. In fact, it washed the whole town away.

"When we landed, we started exploring Alaska, heading north through the mountains until we reached Anchorage. We were sightseeing along the way, and sleeping in the truck. We spent several days traveling back roads in Alaska, making our way up from the Kenai Peninsula. While we were hiking and exploring this remote wilderness, Cassandra was the gun bearer, and responsible for singing loudly so as not to surprise bears.

"At one point, a shrimper came in with a load of king crab, and we got several crabs from them, fresh from the ocean. I scouted around until I found a gallon coca cola can that had been discarded, but was clean, and I heated the crabmeat in butter on that Coleman stove. It was a feast, and I've liked crab ever since.

"We had never seen Mt. McKinley, and we both wanted to. However, we didn't have time to drive to Tok Junction and then up to Fairbanks, which would have been the normal route back then. We decided to drive up the Matanuska Valley, through the Talkeetna Mountains. We didn't have time to get to Mt. McKinley and get back to Texas in time to go to work, but this short cut would give us a view of the mountain from the south. There was no road from Anchorage to Fairbanks in those days.

"The Matanuska Valley was remarkable. Rich, fertile ash soil, with abundant moisture. At that time of year, daylight lasts practically twenty-four hours a day, so vegetables grow to huge sizes—record-breaking cabbages, carrots more than a foot long. We drove through, just marveling at the sights and hoping to get close enough to get a view of the mountain. An asphalt road ran through the valley, but after a while it ended and we found ourselves on a dirt logging road out in the wilderness. When darkness came we were beside a small river. We decided to camp there for the night. We made dinner on our Coleman stove and talked over our plan for the next day. We laughed about a sign we had seen a few miles back, that read, 'Mary's Place: Anything You Want.' We joked about what they might be selling. Then, after supper, we crawled into the truck and went to sleep.

"It started to rain. Around midnight I was awakened by heavy rainfall and a roaring noise I couldn't identify. I sat up and looked outside, and what I saw was that the stream we had camped beside had risen into a raging torrent.

"I got into the cab of the truck, started it up, and began driving back down that timber road toward safety. It was pouring now, and I drove down this increasingly muddy road until finally I got to asphalt, but even driving on the pavement, the water kept shifting the car from side to side. Finally, as I drove out of that valley, Cassandra tapped on the window. I got her into the cab and told her what had happened.

"We drove onto Route 1 and proceeded north. We crossed a bridge and saw that the river below had completely overflowed its banks. We managed to cross the bridge, but after about a mile, we realized we couldn't see the highway. Dirt, rocks, and uprooted trees had washed down the mountainside, and the highway had washed away completely. 'We've got to get back to Anchorage,' I said, and I turned the car around to re-cross the bridge we had left only minutes earlier. The end of the bridge was gone! It had simply washed out. As we watched, giant fir trees were uprooted by torrents of water, and we could actually hear huge boulders washing down the mountain and crashing against the concrete bridge pilings. We were stranded! We couldn't go forward, because the bridge was washed out, and we couldn't go back because the road was washed out. As we wondered what to do, lo and behold, a pickup truck pulled up beside us. The driver called out over the roar of the river, 'Would you like to come to the dog camp?'

"I looked at Cassandra, who shrugged. We didn't have a lot of choices. 'Sure,' I called out, and we began following the pickup.

"It turned out that what he had actually said was, 'Would you like to come to the adult camp,' and as we followed them to a compound of buildings located higher on the mountain, it gradually dawned on us that we were driving onto a prison campus.

202 **To the Max**

We soon learned this was a maximum security prison out in the middle of nowhere. It was the Alaska Maximum Security Prison, now called the Palmer Correctional Center. Our two rescuers were a prison guard named Jim and a prisoner named Ronnie Crabtree. Jim and Ronnie took us to a compound of buildings that were constructed of rock and timber from the mountainside.

"Cassandra and I were escorted to cells in the administration building, where we were assigned a cell of our own to use as temporary living quarters. The main prison building was just a few hundred feet away. We weren't sure what we were in for, but we brought some of our things in, toiletries and such. We were given cots, a place to shower, towels.

"That first night, we stayed up until after midnight, just talking with Ronnie Crabtree, Del Thomas, and an Indian they called Chief. We never did know his name, but apparently these three were prisoner trustees. From the beginning, we ate with the convicts, slept in a cell, and found ourselves getting to know, especially, Del Thomas and Ronnie Crabtree on a human level.

"Ronnie Crabtree was about fifty years old at the time. He was one of those men who got in trouble even as a kid. Cassandra and I could see that he was a con-man, not a violent man—but he had been in and out of detention ever since he was a teenager. He was a habitual criminal. Through long conversations, we found out more about Ronnie's life. One thing we learned was that, when he had been in an Arkansas prison, he told Warden Thomas Murton that some of the trustees who acted as guards had killed other prisoners. He told the warden where the bodies were buried. His testimony was eventually made into the 1980 movie, *Brubaker*, starring Robert Redford.

"So every morning while we were at the prison, Ronnie and Del would meet us and take us to the dining facility, where we would eat breakfast with the prisoners. Cassandra, of course, was young and a former Kentucky beauty queen. But never once did the prisoners ogle her or behave discourteously in our presence.

"However, around the third day we were there, I happened to turn around as we left the mess hall, and every head in the room was craned to watch Cassandra leaving. It had probably been quite a while since some of them had seen a woman."

Meanwhile, the rains continued. After a couple of days at the prison, Max and Cassandra went down the mountain with Jim and Ronnie Crabtree, just to see how things were at the river. Arriving at the end of the washed-away bridge, which now jutted over raging water, they saw that the road on the far side had also washed away. "We saw on the other side of the river that two big D-16 Caterpillar bulldozers had been brought in from Anchorage to clear the debris that was pounding against what was left of the bridge," Max says. "The water was violent, with torrents of water surging off the mountains. We could hear—and feel—massive boulders crashing into the bridge pilings. We were standing at the edge of the bridge as water cascaded off the mountain from hundreds of feet above us, rushing down the mountainside into the Talketta River raging below. And here were these tractors out in the middle of the roiling current, trying to shove debris and uprooted trees away from the bridge. It was clear to see from where we stood that the bridge embankment was washed out and still completely impassable. We saw trees a hundred feet tall washing from the banks and crashing into the torrents cascading down the mountainside. One of the tractors was in the river on the upper side of the bridge. The other was on the down side of the bridge, pushing debris around. Both were in the raging water, on the slope of the mountain. The water roared so loudly we couldn't hear to talk, so we just stood watching them work in these treacherous conditions.

"The down slope tractor was half submerged in the water. As we watched, the driver tried to back it up and move forward to a safer position, but the big machine wouldn't budge. He had the motor at full thrust, and still it wouldn't go forward. Almost imperceptibly then, the bulldozer started sliding backward into the raging water, and we could see the driver yell for help. However, the roar of the water was such that his companion driver couldn't hear. In desperation, the driver put the blade of his caterpillar 'way up in the air and started climbing it. Meanwhile, his caterpillar was slipping backwards into the depths. The driver of the upper caterpillar finally saw the guy, and he started slowly back down to rescue him. The guy on the lower caterpillar kept climbing, until he reached the highest point on the extended blade. The upper caterpillar was making its way down, though progress was breathtakingly slow. It looked doubtful that he could get there in time. As he approached the sinking caterpillar, he lowered his extended blade. The distressed driver jumped onto the blade of his companion D-16, and at the same instant his own caterpillar disappeared into the current. He didn't have one second to spare!"

Through long conversations at the prison, Max and Cassandra learned that Ronnie had written out his entire life history on a yellow legal pad. "He said he had never let anybody read it," Max recalls, "except for a favorite warden. But he wanted Cassandra and me to read it. So we took it to our cell one evening, and we sat down and read it together. It took us several hours, until past midnight, to read the whole story. As we might have expected, he was rebellious as a kid, caused his mother problems, eventually graduated to more serious crimes. I guess it's a common story for people in prison."

Max and Cassandra also spent many hours during those days with Del Thomas. "Del was a young man, very well-groomed, nice-looking, articulate," Max recalls. "He seemed well-read. He kept talking about how he hated to be locked up. Once he said, 'Even dogs shouldn't be locked up.' But he was in for twenty years, and we heard his story, too.

"He had lived on Kodiak Island, having arrived there when his mother moved to Alaska as a single parent years earlier. So he grew up in Kodiak, and when he was of age, he got jobs. Fishing boats, canneries, just whatever was available. The result was that he made a lot of money, but he had no place to spend it, so from time to time he would go to Anchorage for fun. On one occasion, he got to Anchorage with $1,200, a sizable sum in those days. He was planning a weekend of drinking and carousing. He found himself a bar, had a lot of drinks, and teamed up with this young blonde prostitute.

"He and this girl went upstairs to a room. Del eventually went to sleep, and after a few hours he woke up to find his companion and what was left of his $1,200 missing. So he went back to the bar to get his money. When he got there, he started raising hell, hollering about his lost money. A bouncer, a very large black man who was also the prostitute's pimp, threw Del out of the place. Del went back to his hotel room and got a gun, then returned to the bar. He started walking up the stairs to the room where he and the prostitute had been, and the same big bouncer appeared. 'White man, now I'm going to kill you,' he said.

"'No, I don't think you are,' Del said, and he shot the fellow. As he rolled down the steps, Del emptied his gun into him. There would have been grounds for self-defense, but because Del had emptied his gun into the man, he was convicted of murder and sentenced to twenty years. Again and again, Del would tell Cassandra and me that people should not be locked up. He had a real phobia about what was happening to him.

"I remember that Del had been upset when we first got there, because he was scheduled for a parole hearing, and he was afraid this flood would prevent his hearing. The warden and the parole board were not on the premises, and now they couldn't get in because the roads had washed out. After a few days, though, the warden and the parole board members were helicoptered in, which meant that Del would be allowed his parole hearing after all.

"Now Del was excited and nervous. While he was in his hearing, the warden, Ronnie Crabtree, Cassandra, and I were standing around talking and the warden just happened to mention that, in a recent investigation, they had found where a lot of narcotics were. This was a casual conversation, but Ronnie got really excited, saying, 'We've got to go get those drugs. They're worth a lot of money.'

"Right about then, Del emerged from his hearing. Ronnie said, 'Come tell us how the hearing went.' But Del was distraught. He said, 'I can't hardly talk. I've been waiting five years to tell my story. I never had a chance. They only gave me five minutes. I can't talk. I've got to go back to my cell.' So he walked away. I glanced at Cassandra, who had tears in her eyes."

When the roads were clear enough for the Carrs to leave the prison, they went on with their trip. "We got to Tok Junction before it started raining again," Max says. "Now keep in mind that in those days the Alaska Highway was unpaved, 1,100 miles of mountainous road of crushed gravel with sharp edges. Because it wasn't alluvial gravel, it would fly into the air and damage cars as they passed on the road. We hadn't gone ten miles before we had a cracked windshield.

"Eventually I got tired of driving, and I asked Cassandra to take the wheel. We switched positions and I put my head on her lap and went to sleep. It was still raining hard, and that mountainous road was slick. There were no guard rails, even though the roadside fell off hundreds of feet at places. Even so, I managed to fall sound asleep. It's amazing that I could sleep as rain pounded and Cassandra drove treacherous roads cut into the sides of high mountains. Then suddenly I was awakened by her voice, calling, 'Max! Max!' At that exact moment, I could feel the car beginning to slide. I knew that if we went off that road we'd plunge several hundred feet, so I didn't move. I didn't want to disturb Cassandra's reaction. I was aware that the car was starting to slide backwards, and I could hear gravel sliding under the car's underbody. I thought that weightlessness might be my next sensation. Then, miraculously, the gravel sounds began to taper off, and finally they stopped altogether. Very slowly, I sat up and looked out. I saw that we were balanced on the edge of a cliff beside the road. There was nothing but air below us. At any moment the car might slip over the side of the mountain. With extreme care, and quickly, we exited the car. As I stepped away from the car, I saw that it was teetering on the side of the mountain!

"After a time, a vehicle approached. Seeing our El Camino hanging over the edge of the road, the driver said, 'You need a drink!' and he passed me a bottle of whiskey. It turned out these two guys were on the way to White Horse, and they were able to put a chain on the front edge of the car and pull it back onto the road.

"However, just as their truck pulled ours back onto the road, we heard the power-horn of a huge tractor-trailer racing downhill and heading straight for us. The road was narrow, and slick, and he was going fast. When he saw us, he started blowing that earsplitting horn and signaling for us to get out of the way. But of course we couldn't move! The driver had to crash the left side of his truck against the mountain in order to come to a stop, only feet in front of us. He was furious until I explained our situation. After that he was really helpful. When we left, in fact, he gave us some danger flags.

"When we finally got down to hard pavement, we made a beeline to Texas, and we made it home in time to return to work right on schedule. Only sixty miles from home, though, we had a flat. When I investigated, I saw that the entire wheel was split. Pounding on that crushed gravel had completely destroyed our wheel rims."

For a long time after that, Max and Cassandra kept in touch with Del and Ronnie at the prison. They had come to consider the two men friends.

"Because Del was so shaken by his interview with the parole board, Cassandra and I had assumed he didn't have a chance," says Max, "and of course we had to leave before we found out what happened. However, a short time later Del wrote us a letter explaining that he'd been paroled and was working at a gas station in the town where the prison was: Palmer, Alaska. He lived in a small trailer. He said he had no furniture—just a mattress on the floor. He said it was getting colder, but he was fine.

"In his next letter, we learned that conditions had improved for him. He'd gotten an upholstered chair. He was really proud of that chair. Also, he'd gotten a dog for company. Things were looking up for ol' Del Thomas.

"The third letter wasn't quite so cheerful. He said the dog had eaten part of his chair. He sounded glum, but he also said (as he had said before) that he was coming to see us. Cassandra and I were living in Austin at the time. It happened that one morning I was shaving, and listening to the news on the radio. As I half-listened to the announcer, I heard the words, 'Fairbanks. Hi-jacked airplane. Thomas,' and I yelled to the other room, 'Cassandra, I have a feeling Del is coming to see us.'

"Sure enough, we learned that Del had actually hijacked a 747. The reason, he later told us, was that somebody robbed the gas station where he worked. The owner had told Del, 'We know you didn't do it.' But one of the investigators said to him, 'We're going to send you back to prison, because we believe you did this.'

"So Del got drunk, got a gun, and hijacked a plane. On this plane was a U.S. Marshal, who apparently managed to talk Del into giving himself up, after which he wound up with another twenty years. He continued to write us letters from prison. Once he wrote that he'd like a subscription to *Time* magazine, and we sent that to him.

"We stayed in touch with him for a period of time, and for some reason, maybe because he hadn't really committed bodily harm this time, he got an early parole. When we heard that, Cassandra and I sent him money for clothes so he could re-enter society. After that, we never heard from him again."

Cassandra adds with a laugh, "Del said, 'I don't understand why these things happen to me. I only stole one thing, and I gave it back.'"

"As to Ronnie Crabtree, we also communicated with him after we got back," Max says, "usually by letter. At one point we sent him a tape recorder, and we had him read his life story from that yellow legal pad onto a tape. He sent it to us, and we listened to it. It's very honest; in it, he talks about how he caused trouble, even at five years old. Anyway, Ronnie was also given a parole, eventually. He went to California and got a job as a mason. Cassandra and I received letters from him telling us all about his job. Then we got a letter in which he said he had met the most wonderful lady in the world. He described her to us. She was thirty-odd years old, slender, very nice-looking, had blonde hair—and she had $40,000! He was a con man, and we just knew he was going to take her for that money. Then we got another call and they'd gotten married."

"On Valentine's Day," Cassandra says. "During that same call, they said they were coming to Texas to see us."

"But just a short time later," Max says, "Ronnie's new wife called again, and this time it was to tell us that Ronnie was dead. He'd had a job as a tile-setter, and one evening he and two friends stopped to drink a couple of beers. Somehow Ronnie fell at the bar and hit his head, knocking himself unconscious. His two friends took him to the hospital, but the emergency room medics smelled liquor on his breath and assumed he was just drunk and passed out. So his two friends took him home, laid him on the sofa with his hands folded on his chest, and that's the way his wife found him the next morning. Dead."

40

Searching for Gold

After their honeymoon, the Carrs and Ismael stayed in touch. Ismael was lively and engaging, a person of ideas and great enthusiasms. He was always calling the Carrs to report on his latest idea, or, in his words, "thees new opportunity." In the years after their honeymoon, they made several trips to Nuevo Laredo, where they met with Ismael, met his family and went out to eat and drink. Their friendship deepened. In fact, Max was later made godfather of Ismael's youngest child, named Eduardo, after Edward Maxwell Carr. So when Ismael had the idea of opening a bar and restaurant, he felt comfortable in asking Max and Cassandra to buy in. They agreed to be his partners, and Max opened a bank account for Ismael's expenses.

As it happened, though, that money found another use. It all started when an Indian named Sebriano, who lived in the remotest part of central Mexico, discovered a few gold nuggets. An illiterate peasant accustomed to surviving on native intelligence, Sebriano had no idea what to do with his find until, eventually, someone suggested that he travel to Nuevo Laredo and seek money to develop the mine. When he got to the city, he was referred to Ismael, who became so excited at Sebriano's story that he couldn't wait to approach Max and Cassandra with the details. The next day he drove to Austin, as was his habit, and knocked at their door.

Max takes up the story. "It emerged that these gold samples were from a site in the Sierra Madres, a site that was, unfortunately, on government land. Now Ismael wanted to file a claim with the authorities in Mexico City to mine for it, and for this he needed money. His question for us was whether we were willing for him to use the money we'd set aside for the restaurant to finance this long shot. Immediately I remembered—once again—that lost Burmese ruby.

"Ismael's excitement was contagious, so Cassandra and I diverted from what might have been a more sound business decision and took a chance. I remember saying to myself, *Anybody can open a restaurant and bar, but how many people get the chance to mine for gold in Mexico?* I was always up for an adventure. Luckily, so was Cassandra."

Ismael used some of the restaurant money to buy a Dodge pick-up truck, and Max says, "The first thing he did was to have big wheels installed so the truck would make it across the Mexican desert. Then, as soon as the wheels were in place, Ismael took off by himself into remote areas of Mexico.

"At first he would call us every few days, and I could always tell when it was Ismael on the phone, because I'd hear the hollow sound of an open wire lead. During these conversations he would tell us all about what he was doing. He was viewed by the remote Indian peasants as the 'patron.'

"The mine was at an elevation of 8,000 or 9,000 feet, deep in the Sierra Madre Mountains. When I would say I'd like to come down and join him, he would discourage me. 'It is not safe,' he told me. 'The people are so poor they have to steal. The people are hungry and desperate.'

"After a few weeks, though, he called and said he thought it would be all right for me to join him after all. Immediately I loaded my El Camino with goods to give to local people when I got there. I thought this might appease them and make them feel kindly towards me. Besides, Ismael had told me, 'Mr. Max, if someone says he likes your shirt, take it off and give it to him.' With that in mind, I packed some old military boots, binoculars, and various supplies. At the last minute, I decided to pack some peanut brittle candy. Then I headed for Nuevo Laredo, where I met Ismael at the Cactus Café at 5:00 in the morning. We took off for Saltillo, with me following his pick-up in my El Camino. About a hundred kilometers south of Saltillo, near Del Oro, we left the paved road and drove perhaps fifty miles across rough roads until we hit a north-south railroad track that ran all the way through Mexico. From there, we followed dirt roads until they played out after a few miles. The only thing we passed on our way was a little store near the railroad tracks. It was about as big as a closet, and it carried only rudimentary supplies, but we found out we could get gasoline there. However, we had to dip it out of an open container and pour it into our cars. I remember my truck made quite a hit with the locals, who hadn't seen many El Caminos."

Max says Ismael called on local Mexicans when they needed help along the way. Soon after they left the outpost, they passed a tiny village surrounded by a twenty-foot adobe wall. "We saw dogs, javelinas, and lots of naked little kids," Max says. "I realized we were in another world, a throw-back to a previous century. We drove deeper and deeper into central Mexico, until we came to what they called The Ranch, which was actually just a group of adobe buildings located at an altitude of perhaps 7000 feet."

The land here was desolate and dry, with only one well to serve everyone. Ismael pulled over, and Max inferred that this was where Sebriano, the Indian who first brought the gold nuggets to Ismael, lived. "I'd heard that Sebriano was in charge of the ranch because he was the toughest guy around," says Max, "and there was no law in those parts. Sebriano wasn't home when we got to his house, a one-room adobe structure. In one corner of the room, built into the wall, was a triangular, waist-high platform of rock and adobe in the center of which was a blackened oval depression where a fire was smoldering, fed by twigs, with smoke vented through a hole in the ceiling.

"Ismael introduced me to the family: Sebriano's sturdy wife and four children. There was a daughter, Maria, about eighteen; a son, Rogelio, maybe sixteen; and a younger daughter, Mary Lucete, who was only six or seven; and then there was a baby.

"There was a pile of corn stacked in the corner of the room," Max recalls, "and I watched as Sebriano's wife shelled it, ground it with a pestle, and made tortillas on the tin over that central fire. She was a strong-looking woman in her thirties who looked forty-five. She had no shoes. She had a hard life. The youngest of her children was barely old enough to walk, and of course the baby didn't have any shoes, either.

"It was something to see when we started handing out that peanut brittle. It was dusk and the villagers scrambled to get a taste. There weren't many houses, but there must have ten or twelve people lined up for a sample. I looked up while I was passing the candy out, and here was this guy coming off the mountain with a stack of firewood on his shoulders. In his hand, he held a machete. This was my first glimpse of Sebriano. He was walking through country where deadly snakes, mountain lions, and everything else you can name live and thrive, but he appeared completely unaware of danger.

"Ismael told me that a week earlier there'd been a disturbance in the vicinity of the ranch, and Sebriano had gone to settle the dispute. Since there was no law in that part of Mexico, it fell to Sebriano to try to resolve the situation, which involved two guys living in the general vicinity. Sebriano went to see them and he tried to mediate, but apparently he antagonized one of the men. As Sebriano was coming home, he realized the fellow was tailing him, so he hid behind a huge cactus, and when the guy came along, Sebriano decapitated him with a machete. I thought of this as I watched Sebriano approach."

That night, Ismael and Max laid blankets across wooden crates under a little lean-to, and slept there. "The next morning, Ismael and Sebriano and I got into the cab of Ismael's pick-up, while Rogelio and Chinda jumped into the back. Also joining us was a local Indian named Chile.

"Sebriano had a single-shot 22-rifle which we laid on the dash. Then we started out across the desert. Maybe two miles in, we passed some cacti. On one hung a human skull and some other human bones. I nudged Ismael.

"'Look, look.'

"'Si, Mr. Max,' he replied, as though I'd pointed out a jack-rabbit or something. We continued driving for fifteen or twenty miles across the desert, gaining altitude, until we could drive no further. Looking around, Ismael said, 'When God made the earth, he forgot to come here.'

"The roads had played out, so we had to leave the truck and walk. We had a 20-gallon jug of water, and Sebriano threw a loop around that keg and heaved it up on his shoulders. In those days, I worked out a lot, and I thought I was in good shape. In fact, I was pretty proud of my physical condition. I figured I'd show these guys I could be their match. So we set out, and those guys just ran me into the ground. After a few miles of hiking straight uphill, even though I was embarrassed to admit it, I had to tell Ismael that I needed a rest. But the Indians never stopped.

"We finally got up to the site of the gold mine. I saw it was a sink hole, and I concluded that water had washed down the side of the mountain into this crevice or cave, and as the sand washed in, some gold nuggets had washed in with the water. If that was true, obviously the vein of gold itself was somewhere higher on the mountainside.

"We began a search. While the others dug in the mine, I never found the mother lode that I knew had to exist. I planned to try again on a future visit, with better equipment."

Max recalls his fellow travelers vividly. "Chile was a menacing-looking individual with the Indian characteristics of deep-set, piercing eyes, a hawk nose, and waist-length hair. He was in his late twenties, and he looked wild and dangerous. The more I got to know him, the more I realized he lived up to his looks.

"Then there was Chinda, a young man about the same age, who was neat, slender, and really quite nice-looking. Chinda always wore a sombrero, and his hat band had real scorpions sewed on to it. I noticed that he ate very little, and one day I asked Ismael about this. 'Chinda doesn't eat much since a snake got him,' Ismael told me. I asked what he meant, and he told me the story. Chinda's family raised corn, and one day Chinda was plowing his field when he saw a boa constrictor lying across the furrow he was plowing. A nearby mockingbird was raising hell with this boa constrictor. When Chinda tried to move the snake, it somehow wrapped itself around him. He didn't have his machete with him that day, so he took his belt buckle off and decapitated the snake. After that, according to the story, he never ate much; he only drank. Ismael told me this was because the snake had squeezed something inside of him."

Rounding out the group was Rogelio, Sebriano's sixteen-year-old son. "I liked Rogelio," says Max. "On that trip I was wearing boots that were size 10½. Rogelio admired them, so I gave them to him even though he wore about a size six. He wore those boots with pride."

A couple days passed, but the little group didn't find any more gold. One day while we were on the mountain, I asked Sebriano why there was no law enforcement around there. He didn't understand the question until I used the word 'federales.' Then he said, through Ismael's translation, 'Oh, no, Mr. Max. Federales are afraid to come here.'

"I felt as if I'd landed in the 19th Century, and I was fascinated by everything I saw. I wanted Cassandra to be a part of the experience, so Sebriano and I made another trip to that little store. They had a magneto telephone, the kind you had to crank up to use—but somehow I was able to get Cassandra on the line. 'You have to see this,' I told her. 'It's like going back a hundred years in time.' When I finished describing my trip, she said she'd start driving to Mexico the very next morning!

"While we were at the store, I bought Sebriano a new machete, and I also bought some shoes and socks for his baby, who was always barefoot. Then we found the funnel, filled up my truck with gas, and headed back to the ranch."

Cassandra set out from Austin very early the next morning, driving all the way from Austin to Saltillo by herself. "I was driving my white 1965 Chevy Impala," she says. "I didn't have any time to waste. I had to be back at work on Monday, and we had miles to cover in the meantime."

Max says, "Cassandra met Sebriano and me at the Arispe Hotel in Saltillo, and we decided to eat lunch there. Sebriano had a white metal hardhat that he was very proud of. He had it on in this fashionable hotel, and he wore it into the dining room. When I asked him to take it off, he looked puzzled, but he took it off and stored it carefully under his chair.

"As soon as we finished eating, we took off in the El Camino, leaving Cassandra's car at the hotel.

"We got back to the ranch at dusk, and Cassandra met Sebriano's family. The oldest girl, Maria, was speechless to learn that Cassandra was going up to the mine with the men the next day. Maria had never been allowed to go with the men, but because another woman was going, this time her parents decided to let her go."

Cassandra says, "As we hiked through the wilderness, she named all the plants along the way and told us what medical condition each could treat."

"One plant she said was good for impotency," Max adds. "I thought to myself, What does this young Indian girl know about impotency?"

When the group arrived at their destination, the temperature was still blazing hot. "Sebriano saw that Cassandra was uncomfortable," Max says, "and he took his machete and chopped a crevice into the side of a cliff, shading it with branches. I was struck by that. Here was this Indian who would decapitate an adversary, but he was thoughtful enough to want Cassandra to be comfortable."

They didn't find the source of the gold nuggets that had washed into the mine. That was a disappointment, but not enough of one to get in the way of their plans for that evening at the ranch. Max and Cassandra had thought it would be wonderful to have a traditional fiesta to thank the people for their hospitality. To that end, they drove to the outpost store and bought lots of beer, as well as a goat from Chinda and his father. "We watched as two men slaughtered the goat and hung it between two posts," Max says, "and they started to dress it. I had a really sharp fishing knife with me, and I handed it to one of them. It was a well-tooled knife. Watching, I was amazed: in about four or five strokes, they had the hide off that goat. And they prepared every part of that goat for eating. They made a mole sauce and barbecued the cabrito. Also, by the way, they kept the knife.

"It was a great party. People came from throughout the surrounding area. They had on their best clothes. We could see the lines where they'd washed their hands, but forgotten about the dirt on their arms. At one point in the revelry I took a road flare out of my truck, hung it on a tall cactus, and ignited it. In the darkness it was like fireworks. The people were in awe. They'd never seen anything like that before. Someone brought cascarones, the hollow eggs with confetti inside, and the little children burst them on Cassandra's head.

"Almost everybody got drunk. Late that night, as we were all talking and drinking, Señora Cruz, Sebriano's mother, spilled a secret she had never told anyone. She told her son the location of the Lost Monica Mine. She hadn't told him earlier because she was afraid someone would learn that he knew the secret and kill him for the information.

"When Señora Cruz was about sixteen, her best friend had been a local girl named Monica, who married a lieutenant in the Federales army. This officer, who was in charge of all the troops in the area, had been trained in mine engineering, and somehow he determined that there was gold in a certain area. While he was still in the military, he started extracting ore and, with the help of local people, he worked out a crude refining process. The lieutenant then hid the refined gold back in the mine. He thought it would be safe there, because the Indians were afraid to go into the mine unless accompanied by the officers. The Indians were very superstitious, and they didn't want to displease the spirit of the mountain.

"Only a short time after she married the lieutenant, Monica died, and her grieving husband buried her with his gold in the hidden caves. Right away a legend grew around her burial—that she was holding apples of gold, and that at her feet were the golden statues of the Christ. The lieutenant soon died, too, and the location of the mine died with him, except for in the minds of a few superstitious local Indians. It became known as the Lost Monica Mine, and the Indians in the region came to believe that anybody who went into the Lost Monica Mine would die. The few Indians who knew the location began to pass away, except for Señora Cruz, who had been Monica's confidante when they were young girls. She'd known the secret for all these years, and she'd never told anybody.

"But the night of the fiesta, Ismael said, 'Sebriano's mother has told him the location of the Lost Monica Mine. Let's go find it.'"

This opportunity was too much to let pass, of course, so at

midnight that Easter Eve, the tipsy prospectors piled into Ismael's truck, with Max, Cassandra, Ismael and Sebriano in the cab and the rest in the truck bed. The single-shot .22 rifle laid across the dash as they took off in darkness for the Lost Monica Mine. "Sebriano told us more or less where we were going," Cassandra remembers. "Our destination was probably about fifty miles northeast of the ranch, near a place where four Mexican states come together—San Luis Potosi, Zacatecas, Coahuila, and Nuevo Leon."

"Ismael was drunk that night," Max says, "and he was speeding across the desert. At one point Sebriano hollered, 'Alto, Alto!' and Ismael slammed on the brakes. We were inches from the edge of a ravine! He laughed and put the truck in reverse, spinning out as we backed away from the edge. 'Mr. Max,' he said, 'this is something we can tell our grandchildren!' and I whispered to Cassandra, 'If we live through it.'

"Around one in the morning we drove through another isolated settlement. A group of swarthy, mean-looking guys seemed to materialize out of the darkness in front of our truck. Sebriano told them that we were having a fiesta and they were invited. Cassandra and I had bought enough cerveza and food for everyone, and as we drove off, I heard two or three of those guys hop into the back of the truck with Chinda, Chile, and Rogelio.

"When we got to the end of the trail and couldn't drive any farther, we started out on foot. I had a flashlight, and as I picked up the rifle, I thought, *I'm going to ingratiate myself to the meanest hombre in this group*, which was Chile. I handed the rifle to him.

"Chile was a night owl. He seemed able to see in the dark so he took the lead, with Sebriano, who supposedly knew where we were going, right behind him. Behind Sebriano were Ismael, then me, then Cassandra. The rest of them trailed behind in the dark night. There were cacti sharp enough that, if we stepped wrong, the needles would go through the leather of our shoes. As we trudged up the mountain in the darkness, I suddenly had the thought, *Here we are with all these Indians, drunk, far from anywhere. If anything happened to us, nobody would ever hear of us again.*

"After we'd hiked for a while, we stopped and rested, then started out again. At one point Chinda slipped downward off the trail and landed in some cacti, which everybody thought was hilarious. We all had a belly-laugh as he staggered up and got back in line, and then we trudged on. I wasn't sure where we were going. Señora Cruz had described the location to Sebriano, but we didn't have a map and our minds weren't the clearest that night.

"Then suddenly Chile stopped. In the pitch black, we were standing on the precipice of a wide sinkhole. It was so deep that there was a huge tree growing in the floor of it, and the top branches of the tree were fifty feet below where we stood. It was just a tremendous drop-off, and if Chile had taken one more step . . .

"We were standing on a curved rock precipice and we had to lie down on our stomachs to keep from falling in. The floor of this cavernous hole cut back under the rock cliff, in far recesses. I started rotating the beam of my flashlight. Off to the left, the land had washed out and I saw stalactites and stalagmites. The wall was a sheer cliff, and as I rotated the light, I saw a door carved into the recesses of the overhanging rock wall. I looked at Ismael, and he said, 'Si, Mr. Max. We have found the Lost Monica Mine.'

"Also, across the chasm, in a small niche of inaccessible rock cliff, grew a white flower. It was so amazing to see a flower blooming in that dark cavity, but even eerier, it looked like a single white lily and this was Easter morning. It was surreal. Suddenly there was a bright flash of light. At first I had no idea what it was, and I was startled. We all were, until we realized that Cassandra had taken a flash picture of this amazing sight. She and I were still marveling over that flower when all at once, Chile shot the blossom with the rifle. I'm not superstitious, but I thought, *Oh, this is not good.*

"I really wanted to go into that door, but Ismael was listening to the Indians talking among themselves, and he became agitated and nervous. 'No,' he said, 'we must leave. We cannot go in.' He started walking back the way we had come. He whispered, 'Chile says whoever goes in will die. We must go.'

"So we started back, again in single file. I was shining that flashlight in a circle on the ground so Cassandra could see where she was going. After half an hour, the whole procession stopped. Ismael started talking nervously to Chile. 'What is it?' I asked.

"'Chile says we are lost,' Ismael replied. I went to the head of the line and stood next to Chile. I shone the flashlight on the ground in front of him and immediately he took off. He was a full-blooded Indian, born and raised in those desert mountains. I don't know what he saw, or how he did it, but one glance at the lighted ground was all he needed. He led us straight to the car."

The group, more sober now, made its way back to the ranch, and the Lost Monica Mine remained lost.

With the lost Monica mine unexplored, and harboring thoughts and dreams of returning with better equipment for mining, Max knew it was time to leave. "I had become concerned about Cassandra," he says, "and I had the feeling that time and our safety were running out." Too, Max and Cassandra had to be at work in Austin on Monday, so on Sunday they started home. However, their adventures were not quite over. Before they left Mexico, Max would have to call on some of his wartime skills. He explains. "As we drove out of the mountains, Cassandra and I were in the El Camino, following Ismael, when suddenly his truck broke down. He pulled over and I looked at his tires, which were facing in opposite directions! I investigated and found that the socket of his tie rod had broken. His truck was completely un-driveable, and we were miles from any kind of help. I rummaged through the bed of his truck and by pure luck I found a piece of chain, and a nut and bolt. I worked the broken tie-rod back into its socket, tied it together with this piece of chain, and bolted it. This meant the vehicle could at least be steered.

"We had to keep moving, though, so we proceeded until finally we got back to the pavement. At that point, Cassandra and I turned north toward Saltillo to pick up her car, while Ismael turned south in search of a garage to fix his truck."

Cassandra says, "We picked up my car in Saltillo and then caravanned back to Nuevo Laredo. Just before we got there, much to our surprise, Ismael passed us. He had decided not to bother to get the truck fixed.

"By the time we got to Nuevo Laredo, it was dark. Max went through customs first, in his El Camino. I came behind in my

Impala. Max got through quickly, but I raised all kinds of red flags with the authorities. I was in my twenties, I had on green fatigues, and I was tired and dirty. Plus, I'd been in Mexico for just a weekend. I looked like the poster child for a drug trafficker. The custom officials asked me where I lived and I said 'Austin.' That cinched it: they brought out the dogs. They were just sure they were going to find something. They took the back seat out of the car. I was afraid they were going to do a body search. They kept looking at me. I was highly suspect, and no amount of protesting seemed to help. I finally had to point to Max on the U.S. side and say 'That's my husband. He's waiting for me. We came to Mexico at separate times, so we have two cars.' For some reason they believed that. They let me go, and Max followed me the rest of the way home."

41

Doing Business
with Ismael

Within a year after the Lost Monica Mine adventure, a Mexican peasant traveled to Nuevo Laredo one hot day, looking for business partners. He was a poor Indian from the mountains who had come into possession of some gold nuggets, along with knowledge of yet another gold mine in Mexico. The man needed to have the gold assayed and, assuming the quality was high, he needed financial backing so that he could develop the mine. He had been sent to some men in Nuevo Laredo, but these men shot him and, except for a couple of nuggets that he managed to hide, took all his gold.

Gravely wounded, the Indian was brought to Ismael's brother-in-law, a local doctor. The doctor listened to the dying man's story, and called Ismael over to hear for himself. The Indian told Ismael the exact location of the mine.

The next day Ismael showed up at the Carrs' front door in Austin. "I have heard of another gold mine," Ismael told them. "This one is in northern Mexico, in an entirely different part of the country, and now we have another opportunity! Are you interested?"

"I told him I'd want to have the gold assayed before I kicked money in," Max says, "so he left the nuggets with us, agreeing to come back in a couple of weeks. Sure enough, the gold was high grade. The assay report stated that the gold content was profitable for mining, and that the content of semi-precious gems in

221

the sample was even more valuable than the gold. Cassandra and I decided to take a chance again. When Ismael came back to Austin, we told him to count us in. He wanted to know whether we had a *pistola*. 'Why do you need a gun?' I asked him, and he said it was dangerous where he was going, because there was a schoolteacher there who was trying to foment a revolution, and the Federales were out in full force. He said that if he got in trouble, he'd just tell them to 'call Mr. Max.' As a matter of fact, we did have a pistol. So I handed it over and asked him to keep us posted."

Ismael headed out, and about two weeks passed before the Carrs heard anything from him. Max says, "Then one night the phone rang, and I heard that familiar open wire sound on the phone line. I said, 'Hello, Ismael. How's the prospecting?'

"He answered, 'Mr. Max, we are so lucky!' and I thought, *Bonanza*.

"I asked him to tell me about it and he replied, 'I am alive!' The story emerged that Ismael had driven deep into this wild Mexican country, and he'd gotten almost all the way to his destination when he was stopped by the Federales. 'Mr. Max, these Federales were young boys with machine guns,' Ismael told me. 'They were crazy. They asked me where I was going, and I said, "I am the explorer." Mr. Max, the Federales took the pistola from me and said they were looking for anybody who might be involved in the uprising.'"

Max goes on with the story. "Ismael said the Federales released him to stay overnight in a room above a nearby cantina. That night he was looking out the window of his room and he saw the Federales come and take some men, who were just standing on the street below, away in a truck.

"'Where did they take them?' I asked.

"'I do not know,' said Ismael. 'Who knows?'

"Ismael decided to pay for his room for a week so anybody watching would think he was staying, but when he got into his truck the next morning, he just kept driving, all the way back to Nuevo Laredo. He never even got close to the gold."

Max concludes the story with a chuckle. "Cassandra and I agreed, after this second dry run, to put our gold prospecting on hold for a while. But we still dreamed of going back to the Lost Monica Mine sometime in the future."

Returning to their original plans a few months later, Max and Cassandra bankrolled Ismael as he opened the Leopardo Bar in Nuevo Laredo, at the corner of Guerrero and Peru Streets. Says Max, "We were partners in this restaurant, dance floor and bar, and Ismael was proprietor. As often as we could, Cassandra and I went down to visit the place and catch up with him. Through those trips, we got to know his family—his wife and children, his parents and siblings. It was a big, happy Mexican family."

On occasion the Carrs would go out on the town with Ismael and his wife, Yolanda. Max remembers those evenings as spectacular: "The soft light, the mariachis. One night the four of us were in another bar, not his. Ismael had been sampling the tequila. Everybody knew Ismael in Nuevo Laredo. At one point he tapped me on the shoulder and asked, 'Where else could you find this beautiful music for just pennies?' The thing was, they were never *his* pennies. When it came time to pay, Ismael usually disappeared and left me with the bill, which that night was quite a sum," Max laughs.

It became Max and Cassandra's habit to spend time in Mexico whenever they could. They went to Mexico City to attend the medical school graduation of Ismael's brother, Rafael. Cassandra says, "We were included as a part of the family, because we had helped Rafael through med school. But that was a memorable graduation. Max and I thought we were going to a graduation like those we were used to in the states. A speech or two, graduates walking across the stage, et cetera. But it wasn't like that at all."

Max takes up the story. "We were picked up at the airport, and we got into the car with four other people. We drove down Revolution Boulevard until we got to the Isabella Hotel. Cassandra and I had assumed we would be going to a convention center or some large auditorium, where we would sit in long rows of people. Instead, we were guided up to the top floor of this hotel, where we saw two ballrooms, one with popular American music, and one with Mexican music. The rooms were filled with tables, each seating eight to twelve people, and each holding bottles of tequila and whiskey. Everyone was drinking and dancing. At our table was a man from Vera Cruz, a simple man, not an educated person. His son was graduating and he was so thrilled and proud. That was a great day for him."

"We had a huge dinner," adds Cassandra, "and after dinner, there was more drinking and dancing. At one or two o'clock in the morning, when everybody was three sheets to the wind, somebody went up to a microphone and started calling the names of the graduates, but by then everyone was drunk. None of the graduates got his own diploma, but I guess the documents eventually got to their rightful owners. That whole experience was very surprising to Max and me. It was just a big party."

They later attended the Baptism of Ismael and Yolanda's youngest son, Edwardo, named for Max, at a Catholic cathedral in Nuevo Laredo. Max became the baby's godfather.

Then one day the trips to visit Ismael and his family came to an abrupt end. "One morning about 10:30, my secretary told me that somebody had called from Nuevo Laredo while I was in a meeting," says Max. "The caller left the message that Ismael had been shot. I called Cassandra with this news, and then we started making calls to find out what had happened. After a few hours, Yolanda telephoned us and filled us in on the details.

"It seems that Ismael's younger brother had become amorous with a young girl in Laredo. This girl's father and another man, both of whom were deputy sheriffs in Laredo, came looking for Rafael. They came to Ismael's bar, and Ismael drank with these two angry men from 10:00 in the evening until 2:00 in the morning. But Rafael never appeared. After drinking that long, it can be assumed they were all pretty drunk. So they left the bar about 2:00 and went outside, supposedly to talk. But instead, the girl's father shot Ismael. Nobody knows why. We can only speculate. Maybe he shot Ismael because he couldn't shoot Rafael. Or maybe Ismael tried to argue Rafael's case. Or maybe they were mad because Ismael didn't know where Rafael was.

There's no telling what prompted it. They had all been drinking for hours.

"Ismael died early the next morning. We heard from the family that suddenly Rafael was talking to a priest. Apparently he was afraid something was going to happen to him, and he wanted to get right with God.

"As to what happened to our bar and restaurant, things didn't turn out too well. After Ismael died, his wife's brother just took the place over, without any remuneration to anybody. And since they were in Mexico, we couldn't do anything about it. It was our intent that Ismael's wife Yolanda would have the bar as a means of support for her and her children—but her brother took the place away from her. After a time, Yolanda and the children moved—illegally—to Chicago. We stayed in touch for a while. We learned that Yolanda eventually remarried and the family moved to Houston. Today, we understand she is back in Nuevo Laredo, but we've lost contact."

42

Aloft Again

When Cassandra entered Max's life, she was fascinated by his stories about flying. "I loved to hear Max talk about flying. I thought it sounded exciting. I started encouraging him to buy a plane so we could go flying. We could afford it, so why not? We bought our first plane in 1971."

"A friend of ours heard us say that we wanted to buy our own plane," Max says. "He said he knew somebody who wanted to sell an airplane—a guy who needed money to start his business. So we went out to the Tims Airport and flew this little 414-Z. I hadn't flown in a while but my landings were smooth every time. So we bought the plane."

Cassandra recalls, "It was a Beechcraft Musketeer that had been built as a trainer, which meant that I could do all the things from the right seat that he did in the left seat."

"We flew that plane to Kentucky, Boston, and all kinds of places," says Max. "It was a little four-seater that would go maybe 120 miles per hour."

The 414-Z was just the beginning of a long adventure with flying for both Max and Cassandra. Explains Cassandra, "I became more and more interested in flying. Max just had it in his blood to fly, but it didn't come naturally or as a passion to me. I became interested because of him, and he's the one who taught me to fly."

In 1973, she began the formal steps toward getting her license. She says, "I had to fly a certain number of hours with a licensed instructor. That's how we met Richard Levy, another lifelong friend. After that I had to fly solo, and then pass a written test and a flying test with an FAA-certified examiner. I got my license later that same year."

One of the Carrs' good friends and flying buddies is Mark Wells, an AT&T pilot. Mark has flown with Max and Cassandra over the years, and has also been their adviser and sidekick as they've bought and traded planes. Wells recalls, "I met Max and Cassandra through the company. I fly Falcon 900's for company officers and their people. Cassandra was always our favorite passenger. One thing I remember is how patient she was. For example, we once sat on the runway in St. Louis for hours, waiting for the runway to clear because the county didn't have enough money to move the snow. She was a good sport about it.

"The first time I met Max, he came up to the cockpit to meet me when we were on a flight, and he introduced himself as a traveling spouse. He seemed knowledgeable, so I asked him if he flew. He said, 'Yes, I flew in the war.' 'What'd you fly?' I asked, and he named the B-26, C-46. Whoa. I knew immediately that identified him as someone who flew the hump."

Mark Wells and Max were drawn together through a shared love of flying, and soon they started taking long flying trips together. "We flew to Hawaii together," says Mark. "He rode in the jump seat from San Antonio all the way to Oakland, and from Oakland over to Maui. Another time, Max and I flew Max's small plane back from Montana."

Max says, "Mark is a great pilot, with the highest ratings he can get."

Because Max respected Mark's broad-ranging knowledge about aircraft, he naturally turned to him for advice. "Max called me on the phone one day and said, 'Hey I'd like to buy an airplane,'" says Mark. "So I asked him what kind of plane he wanted and he said either a Cessna or a Cherokee, which are single-engine planes. Two days later, he called again and said, 'I bought a plane.' 'Really?' I said. 'What did you buy?' He replied that he had bought a Comanche, which is a twin-engine plane.

Well, this is like somebody looking for a Honda Civic and ending up with a Suburban.

"But I have to tell you, Max is one of the best natural pilots I ever knew. Some people are just like that. In the war he flew ADF, or Automatic Direction Finders. This is an antiquated system, and nobody uses it any more. I tried to teach him VOR, or Very High Frequency Omni Range, but he didn't want to learn it. He just used Distance Measuring Equipment (DME)—but they were phasing those out, you see. Around this time the new Global Positioning Service equipment (GPS) was coming into wide use, and we looked at handhelds, and finally Max bought one of those. He liked that method of navigation. He had his own system, and it relied heavily on instinct.

"Eventually, though, he had to sell the Comanche plane, which was 180-200 mph airplane, because Cassandra couldn't ride in it. She was an officer of the company by then, and she was required to ride in company planes.

"Only a few months passed, however, before Max decided to buy another plane, and this time he called me and asked me to help him look around. I said I'd be glad to, but two days later he called again and said he'd already made a purchase. This plane was a Cherokee. He enjoyed flying that plane, and a year later we were all in New Braunfels and we saw a Bonanza, which is a six-person plane. Max said, 'Hey, how about that one?' So we went shopping for a Bonanza and we found one in Dallas and bought it for him. It was in gorgeous condition. He had both the Cherokee and the Bonanza at one time.

"His next plane was a Maule, which he bought after he sold the Cherokee and the Bonanza. On June 5-6, 2004, he and his friend David Berry flew the Maule to Montana and left it there to use. The next summer he decided he wanted to bring it back to Texas. I went up to fly it back with him. June 6-7, 2005, were the dates. It took us two days to get that plane back to Texas, and that was one of the best flying trips I'd ever had. Day one we were in Bozeman. We'd been watching the weather and it wasn't too bad, but it wasn't great. We needed to go through a pass near Bozeman. Since we had marginal weather, we were going to fly on instruments. The plane held about ninety gallons of fuel, but the elevation there was 4,000–5,000 feet. The problem was that the plane would not fly that well with so much fuel, and we had to fly at 10,000 feet to get across the pass. Max had a friend there who said you could get through at 8,000 feet with a visual field. We could see the ground and we were between clouds, and we were flying VFR, or Visual Flight Rules.

"So we got through the pass okay and we headed toward Billings. We were on top of the clouds. We decided to go all the way to Sheridan for a fuel stop. However, I got on the radio and learned that there was a tornado warning for Sheridan. Now we had to figure out where to stop. We had a hundred miles on our left and a hundred miles on our right with thunderstorms, and straight down the middle it was clear. Somehow we got all the way to southeastern Wyoming and that's where we stopped, in the town of Douglas. We had some serious headwinds. In Wyoming there were cars on the highway that were passing us as we were flying. But that flight was gorgeous because of the clouds. Just the top of the peaks sticking out, and a thunderstorm on either side of us.

"We fueled up in Douglas and flew to Goodland, Kansas, to stay all night. Everything there was closed, but we managed to get a room at a Howard Johnson's. The next day we got up and all the weather was behind us, and we flew from Goodland to Mineral Wells, fueled up there and flew the rest of the way to Austin. The main thing I remember about that flight is that the aircraft did not have autopilot in it, but Max could hold that plane steady as a rock, not waver one bit. He is one of the best instinctive pilots I've ever known. He's a complete natural. That's a talent you can recognize right off the bat. As soon as you see him flying, you understand this guy knows what he's doing. I've always admired that about him."

Max says his early training helped hone those instincts. "Going through flight training when I did was extremely hard. The military intended it that way. They figured if they could break you, it was better to do it in training than in combat. So they *tried* to wash you out. But my fellow pilots always said that if anybody could make it, I could. It has helped keep me steady ever since."

"Even the last flight I had with Max, he had control," says

Mark Wells. "It was in the late fall of 2005 when Max and I flew to Boerne to sell his plane there."

"I didn't know it at the time, but my depth perception had changed," says Max. "I bounced the hell out of that plane as I landed. I hadn't realized I had an eye problem until then."

"That's the only bad landing I ever had with Max," says Mark. "I knew something must be wrong. You see, Max never tells you if something is wrong. Here's a story that illustrates what a good pilot he is. Max went over to Hondo with a buddy, and apparently a wasp had built a nest in the carburetor, reducing the engine to half-power. Max realized something was wrong and decided to fly back to the strip at Hondo. After he turned around, he approached some wires and realized that he would have a very hard time clearing them. So he flew in between the ground and the wires, did a complete turnaround, and brought the aircraft back to land it. He just flew at a lower altitude until he could land. To do this, he had to calculate ground effect. What is ground effect? Say the plane's wingspan is thirty-five feet, and the plane will stall at fifty miles per hour. If you get below thirty-five feet, you can fly at a few m.p.h. slower without stalling. He had to figure all that out in an instant in order to fly between the wires and the ground, and bring that plane in safely."

Because Max seemed almost to stumble into flying, with very little forethought and only a vague desire to impress a girl he was dating, his close friends and family members have often speculated on his remarkable ability as a pilot. His cousin, Eugene, has a theory. Eugene says, "Back in 1932, a dirigible was built by Goodyear. It was the first such vehicle ever, and it was called the Akron Airship. There was a huge hangar for it at the airport. It was just enormous. Its doors opened onto railroad tracks, and those doors were so big and heavy that it would take five minutes just to open one. On the day they christened the Airship Akron, my family happened to be visiting Max's family. And we all went out to the airport to see that airship christened. Amelia Earhart was there, and she was flying in a gyro-plane, which was a regular airplane with a propeller like a helicopter. Earhart came in and left on that gyro-plane. We got to see that.

It was a big day. I always wondered if that might have made an impression on Max, and made him want to fly. You just never know when these ideas are planted. But no question, Max has a talent for it."

43

Cassandra Rising

When he talks about his wife, Max Carr's eyes light up. He is a modest man who wouldn't think of bragging on himself, but he can't find enough superlatives to describe Cassandra. "She is the most remarkable person I've ever met," he says, "man *or* woman. It's rare for someone to be smart, beautiful, and accomplished and not have a big head. But she doesn't. Cassandra has met the Queen of England, United States presidents, CEOs, as well as janitors, cooks, drivers. Whoever she meets, though, her approach is always the same. She is gracious and personable.

"Cassandra has always worked well with people, and consequently her career at Southwestern Bell covered a rise from newly hired college graduate, through the ranks to a position just below the chairman of the corporation. She definitely broke the glass ceiling for women in that company."

Given the twenty-five year difference in their ages—Max was fifty when they got together, and Cassandra twenty-five—it's fair to wonder how their families reacted to their marriage. Says Max, "My family was fine with it. Everybody loved Cassandra right from the start, because of her wonderful personality."

Cassandra's family, on the other hand, didn't even meet Max until after he and Cassandra were married. "Her family knew very little about me prior to her calling and telling them we'd gotten married," Max says, "but soon after the wedding, we went to visit her parents and her sister and brother-in-law in Louisville. I remember I took one of my paintings with us to her parents' house. It was a painting of a cow skull in the desert, and there was a vulture sitting on top of it. As I think about it now, I guess that wasn't the most romantic of themes. Her dad asked her—not in my presence—'What can he do besides painting these pictures?' When Cassandra told me that, I realized the jury was still out on me.

"I know her parents must have had trepidation, but everybody was affable. I guess her parents understood by then that Cassandra was the kind of person who was going to make her own decisions. I always emphasized the value of harmonious relationships with her parents and also her paternal grandmother, who was still alive at the time. It was wonderful to see, through the years, the love that grew between them."

Max's affection for Cassandra's family has also deepened during the thirty-seven years of the Carrs' marriage. "As time passed, I came to believe that her family accepted me, but I didn't know for sure until recently, when Cassandra's mother, Irene, remarked that if Cassandra had it all to do over again, that she hoped she would marry me. This was meaningful to me because it was coming from a woman who is only six months older than I am."

Cassandra adds, "Actually, Mom accepted Max immediately. As soon as he walked in the door on that first visit, Mom said, 'I always knew you would marry somebody who loved baseball and basketball.' And the funny thing is, Max didn't know anything about either sport."

"Right, but I sure learned!" Max adds. "I just hadn't realized that loving sports was a requirement in the Colvin family."

Since Max and Cassandra were both telephone company executives, how did they avoid competition in their marriage? "We've always had a high trust level," Max says, "by which I mean we each have confidence in the other's ability to make good decisions. This has affected all phases of our life together. Consequently, there has never been mistrust between us. I think of our marriage as a partnership—both personal and in the business world. By the time Cassandra came into my life, I had already been up to the plate and swung at the ball and I was content with where I was—in life and within the company. At the time, I was a seasoned old-time employee, so to speak, and Cassandra was on the fast track. The ladders of opportunity lay ahead for her. After we married, the telephone company was very considerate about trying to provide positions for both of us in order to accommodate Cassandra's promotions. With each major advancement, though, she was required to move. That's when it became evident to me that this would be a good time for me to retire. What I wanted most at that point was to help Cassandra develop to her fullest ambitions. I knew that as she did, I would have the vicarious pleasure of her achievements. So I retired on December 31, 1983. By coincidence, the divestiture of AT&T took place the next day, on January 1, 1984.

Cassandra says, "The irony of Max's retiring so that we could move for my jobs is that, throughout his career, he had chosen not to move."

"That's true. My decision was based on coming out of the war and wanting only peace and tranquility. I thought there was too much upheaval in higher levels of management, and I was content with my position in the company. My main career goal after the war was simply to have a good life."

"Many of us who know Max can't help speculating on how far he would have risen in the company if he had been willing to move," Cassandra muses.

The Carrs moved to Washington, D.C., where Cassandra was to participate in a program run by the Conference Board. She explains. "The Conference Board took people from multiple businesses, such as Alcoa, GM, and others, and assigned each of us to a job on Capitol Hill. I was on loan to the House Ways and Means Sub-Committee on Trade for a year. The idea was to open up lines of communication between government and corporate America. This experience made me much more valuable to the company, because I came to understand more about how government works."

Max and Cassandra had a wonderful time that year in Washington, and when the assignment was over, in December

1986, Cassandra was named to a government relations job in St. Louis. They moved to the Mid-West.

In St. Louis, Cassandra continued doing regulatory work, but at the corporate level. "I was able to use the knowledge I had gained in Washington in that position," she says. In 1988, she became Senior Vice-President of Finance for SBC Communications, Inc.

Meanwhile, the newly retired Max took up golf, painted, and finished out the basement of their house. "The house had a raw basement," Max says, "and I made it into a rec room. I also enjoyed working out at the gym three times a week. Cassandra and I had a good time in St. Louis."

"It was a good time for me professionally," Cassandra says. "Becoming an officer of the company was a huge step forward for me. I was working for Ed Whitacre, who became the chairman designate of the company"

Max adds, "This was 1988, and it's notable that Cassandra was the first female appointed to this level of management. She really paved the way for other women to enter higher levels of management."

The Carrs stayed in St. Louis until December 1990, at which time they returned to Austin. "Back in Austin, I became President of the Texas Division of the company," Cassandra explains.

In 1994, the Carrs moved to San Antonio, where Cassandra became Senior Vice-President of Human Resources. She continued at that level until 1998, when she was named Senior Executive Vice President-External Affairs. The Carrs bought a home in the Dominion, on the golf course, where they lived until Cassandra retired in 2002.

The Carrs are the first to admit that the telephone company has been something of a third partner in their marriage. Explains Max, "We talked about work a lot. At night we would discuss different issues from the office. I know that it's because of Cassandra's personal capabilities and ambitions that she has been able to be highly successful, but the managerial knowledge that I've gained through years of experience has also been useful to her. I shared what I knew through our conversations.

"Cassandra has always wanted to prove that women have as

much business capability as men do. She certainly established that in her own career, as she advanced through the levels to executive management in the phone company. Right before she retired, her title was Senior Executive Vice-President. When she held that position, people finally stopped questioning whether women could compete. But before Cassandra, it wasn't that way. There was a great deal of prejudice toward women. Cassandra was a forerunner, a pioneer in telecommunications. Other women have followed. Several women who worked for Cassandra at various times over the past thirty years now occupy positions of authority in the company. That's because Cassandra broke the glass ceiling. Nobody would argue with that. She was one of the most respected and admired women in telecommunications."

After Max and Cassandra had been married for a few years, and when they were back living in Austin, Cassandra decided to enter graduate school at the University of Texas. "She got a Master's in special education," Max says. "She attended classes while she was working for the phone company, and she finished with a 4.0 average. She never had in mind to change careers, to teach or work with people with learning disabilities. She always knew she would stay in business, but at that point she wanted more in her life than just working, and she thought that furthering her education would enrich her life. That's my take on it. She earned the degree in her off time from a high-level job."

Max claims that he and Cassandra rarely disagree. "In more than thirty-five years of marriage," he says, "we have never had an argument. And there's a reason for that. We agreed that if either one of us was upset, we would go to the other and say, 'I have a problem.' In consideration of each other, we have always been able to resolve any problem that arises without a breach in our relationship. That's really true. I don't remember a time when we have gotten mad, had harsh words, sulked. That has never happened. Our consideration for each other has made our marriage successful. I'm proud of Cassandra. I admire her. And I'm not bashful about my feelings for her."

Their moves were interesting and sometimes exciting, but the Carrs had become attached to the Texas Hill Country. "As I look back over our married life," says Max with a smile, "I would say that Cassandra and I were happy everywhere we lived, and we found good things about each place. But it's easiest to be happy in Texas."

After Cassandra's retirement, the Carrs returned to Austin, where they bought a beautiful stone home in a gated community with a terrific view of the lake and the hillside. Cassandra went to work for a company headquartered in Austin, Public Strategies, Inc., the company founded by the Carrs' close friend Jack Martin.

Max and Cassandra Carr soon after their marriage on November 27, 1970.

Max first met Cassandra's family in December 1970, on a trip the newlyweds took to meet each other's families.

Max with his brother, Glenn Carr, on that trip.

Max and his sister, Mary Louise.

Left to right: Max's cousin, Eugene Brannon; Max's aunt, Gay Brannon; and Max, in Kenna, West Virginia.

Here, Max visits his sister Juanita and his brother Ford.

Max with his Aunt Gay at her 100th birthday party.

Max's grandchildren, left to right, Jodi, Colton, Josh, Tobi, Sasha.

Max with machete at "the ranch" in Mexico.

Señora Cruz, Sebriano's mother

Señor Cruz

Children at Fiesta with cascarones

Looking into the Lost Monica Mine: (foreground to background) Sebriano, Ismael, Max, Chinda

Luis Eduardo's baptism, with (left to right) Ismael, Yolanda, Cassandra, and Max

Max teaching Cassandra's nephew, Rick Weller, how to fly. The Beechcraft Musketeer 414Z was one of Max's favorites. It's the plane he used in teaching Cassandra to fly as well.

Cassandra and Max at their going-away party, given by Southwestern Bell friends in 1985, when they moved from Austin to Washington, D.C.

Max with his pilot friend, Mark Wells.

Christmas 1999 at the Carrs' house in San Antonio. Left to right: Max, Irene Colvin, Jean Ann Ford Knox, Nancy Morgan, Rev. A. B. Colvin, and Cassandra.

Celebrating Max's 88th birthday: Left to right: Max, Hazel Harris, Dennis Harris, Cassandra.

44

Travel Snapshots

One thing the Carrs decided early in their marriage was that they would explore the world together. To this end, they set a goal of taking a three-week vacation outside the United States every other year.

Max says, "My attitude was that, if I've already been to a place once, I'm not going to go back. I want to see something different."

"We did manage to take international trips as planned throughout our marriage, all the way up to the time we bought our place in Montana," adds Cassandra.

The Carrs managed to visit places that were historic, or exotic, or just plain fun. A few accounts of these trips follow.

"Cassandra and I went to Hong Kong," says Max, "and one day we took the ferry over to Macau. We traveled by bus, about fifty miles in. One young Chinese girl talked to us about life there. I saw out the window that the roads and farm implements were the same as they had been during WWII. Farmers still used the old three-wheel farm vehicles. In fact, there were no signs of modernization except for the omnipresent television antennas. I told Cassandra that those television sets were going to change China."

"In the early 1970s, Cassandra and I were visiting her

248

mother and dad in Hawaii," Max recalls. "Rev. Colvin was an interim pastor on Maui then. While we were there, I got to know a local Hawaiian named Taco, and one day he and I were in the ocean adjacent to a jungle seashore. Taco was teaching me how to use the circular cast-nets. After a while, we got tired of throwing the net and decided to take a swim, and also dive down to search for unusual sea shells. I remember Taco cautioned me to avoid the coral reefs, because they were sharp and would cut my hands to ribbons.

"After my first dive, I surfaced and saw that Taco was staring into the near distance. Following his gaze, I spotted several shark fins in the water. Not being that familiar with sharks, I asked Taco if we had a problem. He looked at me and smiled. 'I don't,' he said. 'They just like white meat.' I got the message. We swam to shore and got out of the water pronto."

"Cassandra and I were down in Rio, walking on the square next to Ipanema Beach. It happened to be election day. As we strolled along, I suddenly heard a sharp clap. I thought it was a firecracker until this guy ran past us, half bent over, with a Lugar in his hand. I realized that what I had just heard was a shot.

"Other shots followed. It emerged that two rival gangs were having a gun battle with each other, and we were standing right in the middle of it.

"There was a bank building to our right and I noticed some heavy windows fronted by a limestone ledge. I pulled Cassandra behind that so we could watch the action from a position of protection. At our hotel, we had been warned not to wear any jewelry on the streets. We were told that gangs had divided Rio up for crime purposes.

"As we watched, one guy was shot. Soon we heard the police coming, and everybody scattered. The wounded man was dragged into a drug store. Eventually the police hauled him back out and took his body away. That was the last we saw of him. Eventually, Cassandra and I emerged from our hidden spot and went on our way."

After Max retired from the military as a Colonel, he and Cassandra were eligible to fly space-available on military transport. They enjoyed several trips by this means. They both remember the first such adventure.

"We were living in Austin," Max recalls, "and we planned to go to England via military transport. We got some English money and got ready to head out. This was the first time we had ever flown military space-available."

Cassandra explains, "In those days, trips weren't computerized, so we went to Bergstrom, signed our names, and then waited. Twelve hours passed, fifteen hours. As flights came and went, the man on the loud speaker would call the names that had risen to the top of the list. Of course, there were other people waiting with us. When our name was finally called, the plane was going to Spain, not England. We'd been waiting so long that we decided to be spontaneous and head for Spain. We wound up landing in Madrid, with no Spanish money. Only English money. After we landed, we couldn't even get off the base until we had procured a visa. So we changed our plans accordingly. We ended up traveling three weeks without an itinerary. We'd wake up in the morning and decide what we wanted to do that day." She laughs. "From Madrid we went to Barcelona, where we stayed in a brothel. It was listed at the train station as a two-star hotel."

Max says, "We said we wanted to stay in all the least expensive hotels. We wanted to see what that was like. The hotel where we stayed in Barcelona had red lights and wallpaper. And we could hear noises from other rooms. Giggling and shouts."

From Barcelona the pair took a train to Milan, to Zurich, to Geneva. After Switzerland, Germany. Cassandra says, "We were both working then, and I had to be back at a certain time. Max and I realized we wanted to spend some time in England before returning home, so we needed to leave the continent immediately. We didn't have time for a bus or ferry. We had to fly from Garmisch, Germany, to England.

"Meanwhile, Max had gotten sick, so he stayed in the room while I went downtown and found a travel agency to buy airline tickets to London. I was given a price of $1,100 each. I said,

'That's ridiculous.' But we had to get back. Finally, the travel agent said, 'You need to talk to the man in the back room.' So I went into the back room and told this guy my predicament. He proceeded to explain the process of riding on a charter rather than a commercial airplane. He said he had deals where we could get a round-trip to London with four nights in a nice hotel for only $400 apiece. 'You just give me cash and pick up your tickets at the airport,' he said. So with misgivings I gave the man $800 and left with no tickets and absolutely nothing to show for my money.

"I got back to the room and told Max what I'd done. We had no choice but to go ahead with the plan, so the next morning we headed for the Munich airport. Sure enough, as we were walking through the door, we heard an announcement: 'Mr. and Mrs. Carr, please proceed to gate so-and-so to get your tickets.' We boarded a brand new plane, and it was equipped with automatic landing. Completely hands-off."

Max adds, "We didn't know that this was the first time they'd used their automatic landing until we met one of the pilots in the terminal, who told us. It was a very smooth landing.

"We got to England in time enough to get a car and drive to Stonehenge and Bath. And then we took a ferry to Ireland. We looked around Dublin and then flew back to Manchester, England. On that trip we met so many kind strangers. For example, we wanted to take a bus to Stratford, but we didn't have English money—only Irish. So the people on the bus took up a collection to pay our fare. It didn't stop there. One person even got off the bus and stayed with us until we could arrange transportation, which was a phaeton taxi. The cab driver drove us the forty miles or so to Stratford-on-Avon, and then drove us around until we found a place to stay. He first took us to a Bed & Breakfast that didn't have room for us, and kept with us until he found us a room in a fantastic B&B."

First stop in Australia. Cassandra makes friends with a koala bear.

On the train in Australia

White water rafting in New Zealand

Max at Machu Picchu

Max and Cassandra celebrate Max's birthday in Peru.

Celebrating Cassandra's birthday in Argentina.

With grandson Josh in Norway

On a trip with grand-daughter, Jodi, to Cozumel. Their original plan was to visit Monterrey, but the flight was canceled, so they went to Cozumel instead.

Cassandra's niece Anne proves that Max washes his clothes along the way—this time in Vienna, Austria.

Max on an Alaskan cruise with Cassandra and granddaughter Sasha

45

Montana

In October 2001, Max and Cassandra were visiting good friends Max and Gene Alice Sherman at their summer home in Montana. The Carrs liked the area so much that they immediately started looking for property of their own. With the help of a realtor, they searched a two-hundred-mile radius of Livingston, and on their third visit to the area, they first saw the Jumping Rainbow Ranch.

"We both really liked it," says Max. "From the top tier, the overview that you get of the valley and the river and the mountains is simply gorgeous."

"It was wonderful just to be in that area, with the mountains and the Yellowstone River," Cassandra agrees. "Our realtor told us of an old trapper who had walked every foot of that river, and he always claimed that the ranch was the prettiest place on the Yellowstone. At the lower elevation, it stays green all year. Actually, scenes from the movie 'A River Runs Through It' were filmed on parts of the Jumping Rainbow Ranch."

"The East River Road leading to the ranch is the oldest road leading to Yellowstone National Park," says Galen Ibes, the previous owner of the ranch and now the Carrs' close friend, "the first road ever built here. The ranch is situated in a tiered Valley between the Absaroka Mountain range and Gallatin Range. It's a beautiful spot."

Max and Cassandra decided to buy the ranch and convert the lodge to a private residence.

Today, the Carrs spend several months a year at Jumping

Rainbow Ranch. Usually their house is full of friends and relatives. Max's granddaughter, Sasha Hobbs, had her wedding on the banks of the Yellowstone River in front of the ranch house in the summer of 2006, and the whole family attended. There's plenty of room. There is even a charming "bunkhouse"—actually a two-bedroom, one bath cottage with a comfy kitchen.

"That's what we wanted Jumping Rainbow Ranch to be," Cassandra says. "A comfortable, welcoming place for our friends and family."

As is Max's habit, he continually sees ways of improving the property. One problem the Carrs face at the ranch is that of erosion.

Galen explains. "After one of those big floods, water ate away twenty feet of the bank going toward the lodge. So Max came up with a plan for reinforcing the shores of the river by hauling in rocks and root wads to keep erosion down. Later he studied the ponds and the way the creek ran, and he decided to change it. He ended up revamping the existing pond, removing some ponds, building up some creeks, and changing the way the water dumps into the river. There was also a little creek behind the lodge, and Max studied that in order to make it possible for the fish to swim up from the river into the water on the ranch to spawn."

"While he was at it, Max decided a little pond just outside the back of the house would be nice. So we built one, about 50' by 50'. Max calls it 'Cassandra's pond.' "

"I've always been interested in the way water flows," says Max. "I seem to have a sense for how to redirect it to best advantage. The ranch gave me an opportunity to try some of my ideas out."

The land in Montana has another, almost mystical pull for Max, through a shared family history that stretches back two generations—and also forward two generations. On a recent rainy summer day, walking the periphery of the Jumping Rainbow Ranch, Max explains. "In 2006, there was a terrible forest fire while we were in Montana," he says. "The fires were not in our area, but there was so much smoke that it became difficult to breathe. Therefore, Cassandra and I decided we would drive out of the valley to find a place where there was fresh air. We left the ranch without a destination in mind, heading north-west. We drove maybe 150 miles, and by then it was getting dark. We needed to stop, and we saw that Helena was right ahead of us. We decided to spend the night there.

"I said to Cassandra, 'You know, this is the location where I've always been told that my grandfather came, when he had to leave West Virginia. He died alone up here. Why don't we see if we can find his grave?' Other people had come looking for it, but no one in the family had ever been able to find it.

"Cassandra and I went down to the state capitol building where we told the receptionist what we were trying to do. She directed us to a small building nearby, where historical records are kept. We went there and repeated what we were looking for. The receptionist there handed us several books that mapped out graveyards in the vicinity. These were record books listing people who had expired there in the past. We started looking through them, and the lady who worked there became interested in what we were doing. Soon, she found some older records that listed Grandfather's name. This list indicated that he died of consumption in the 1890s, and that he was buried in the Odd Fellows Cemetery. So Cassandra and I drove out to that historic cemetery. We walked around and read every gravestone in the place, but we could not find his name.

"We began to think we had struck out. But there was another cemetery across the street that was still in use, and on a whim we went there and talked to a lady. She listened, then said, 'Wait a minute.' She turned around and opened up a stand-up safe, where she found a small, really old and dusty volume of some type. We leafed through it and we found Grandfather's name. Not only that, but she told us what part of the cemetery he was buried in. She said she wanted to go with us, and together we found the unmarked gravesite. Then she called the cemetery caretaker, who said, "Stay there a few minutes. I'll be right over." So the caretaker came, and when we met him, we told him we wanted to put a headstone on the grave. He took us into town and we made arrangements for a headstone to be made and placed on Grandfather's grave.

"Therefore, more than a hundred years after he died alone in Montana, Grandfather's family finally found him, and he got a marker. It seemed to me that life had come full circle, as his great-great-granddaughter married only a few miles from the place where he died. A century passed between those two events in my family."

A gentle rain begins as Max walks up the slope toward his and Cassandra's beautiful mountain home. "I love the rain," he says. "I love to get out and walk in it. I always feel amazed to be walking in the rain here, where it's beautiful and safe."

He gestures toward the river and then his gaze turns upward, toward the mountains, "It's a kind of Utopia. I know that." He falls silent, taking in the beauty. A long moment passes. "I'm a lucky man," he says.

The Carrs' home in Montana, the Jumping Rainbow Ranch, in Paradise Valley.

Afterword

My husband, Max Carr, leaves every place and person he comes in contact with better off because of the encounter. Whether it's the waitress at this morning's breakfast or the grandchild he has watched grow up, everyone benefits from Max's life experiences, generosity, and ability to teach in any situation.

No telling of his life would be complete without mention of the impact he has had as wise counselor and mentor to so many. Examples include several relatives and friends who have, at times, been invited to live with us. Some stayed a few weeks, some for as long as two years. These young people all feel close to Max, and continue to seek his counsel regarding important decisions and events of their lives.

So whether through a chance encounter or a live-in experience, Max has become mentor to many. As Jean Ann Knox puts it, "Max has given us so many sermons, we joke that we should number them!" Following are examples in just two areas.

On education:

Max's granddaughter, Sasha Hobbs Harrison, sums it up, "I'd say Granddad's biggest influence on me was in encouraging me to get a good education. I'm working on an MBA now because he encouraged me to go back to school. Also, he's paying most of my tuition."

My nephew, Rick Weller, says, "I think Max stresses the value of education because he didn't get to have an education himself.

He and Cassandra really encourage people to go to college. They've helped a lot of us with our expenses." Rick also recounts how Max taught him to play pool starting when Rick was only five or six years old. Later, Rick noticed that he was a lot better at pool than his friends and he knew that was because Max was a good teacher. "I'm sure that seeing the value of a good teacher at such a young age shaped who I am now: a teacher."

Jodi Hobbs Welker, another granddaughter, was the first to live with us. She recalls that education was the reason she came into our home. "I lived with Max and Cassandra during my freshman and sophomore years of high school," she says, "so I could go to a small private school with high academic standards, where every child gets a lot of attention."

Grandson Josh Hobbs admits, "Despite Granddad's best efforts, I never did become academic in my focus, but mechanically I learned so much from him when I lived there. I was interested in building things and I learned fundamentals, such as using saws and working with wood. Granddad would go to repair or build something and he would take me along."

Anne Weller Waggoner, my niece, reflects on Max's position on education by saying, "Max has taught me the value of education, but it's more complicated than that makes it sound. Max definitely tries to instill in people the value of a formal education—going as far to offer the 'Carr scholarship.' I have heard him speak many times about the need for higher education to get ahead in society. However, he has also taught me that formal education is not everything. Max, as far as I know, had only a few classes past high school, yet he is one of the more 'educated' people I know. I think this is both an innate gift and the result of his seeking out information and observing the world closely. He has taught me that formal education is valuable only when paired with curiosity and a lifelong desire for learning."

On personal success:

Jean Ann Knox was the recipient of considerable career advice when she entered the business world. "Max always told me I couldn't just stay with the pack. I had to be ahead of the pack.

And no one would do it for me, he said. I had to do it for myself, no matter how hard it was."

On a more tactical level, Max advocated ways to be accepted in business and social circles. Nancy Morgan, a good friend, remembers that Max advised her to "Listen, ask questions and find the subject that engages those around you. People like to talk about themselves."

Jean Ann remembers another "sermon" she puts into practice. "Don't make things personal when you're making a business decision. Take the personal aspect out of it. Learn to be objective."

My cousin Nathan Martin says one lesson had a big impact on him. "Max would say, 'Don't try to impress people with talk.' He believed that, instead of talking about how difficult something is, a person should just do the hard thing. He told me people are far more likely to respond to actions proving a person's worth than to words that try to validate it."

These snippets give only a glimpse at the breadth and depth of Max's influence. Even though some of his favorite experiences—such as flying airplanes, or taking extended foreign trips—are no longer options, his skills at teaching and "sermon" delivery are finely honed and always at the ready.

—Cassandra Carr
2008

Appendix

Positive Management Speech

By Max Carr

Our discussion today involves your role as a manager in the Southwestern Bell Telephone Co. We will be looking at a few facets of supervision, basically those in the area of positive leadership and discipline.

So that we may start thinking along the same lines, please consider these questions. Do troublesome problems exist on your job? Is your job affected by a lack of positive leadership?

Why do we begin with this bit of self-analysis? The first steps of effective leadership are to critically review your own performance, identify your deficiencies and take steps to correct them. If you can see no problems, then you are either an outstanding manager or you and your boss are in trouble and you don't realize it. If inefficiencies are recognized in your operations, then there is a good likelihood the cause is non-competitive type management. If some employees in your operation are not adequately trained, if communications are poor, if results are below objectives and procrastination is not only tolerated but has become standard operating procedure, then it follows that you have need for improved leadership.

Why this discussion? Frankly, we see evidence that some management employees are not living up to the full moral responsibility of their job. We recognize an inclination to avoid conflict. We also recognize the impossibility of maintaining flabby management and weak managers in the present era of inadequate earnings and troublesome operating results. To improve our business, we must better the performance of all employees. To better the performance of our employees, we must improve the quality of our supervision. It is our intent to hold their boss accountable for their results, both good and bad, and treat them accordingly.

You must provide the type of leadership that will motivate employees to get the best out of their skills and abilities. You must radiate confidence and create an instant image of our competence. You must have the moral courage to meet conflict and take steps to eliminate roadblocks to success. Am I saying, "Create conflict?" I am not. Do I prescribe hard-boiled management? The answer is a definite no. But I do place a priority call for aggressive, competitive management.

A supervisor may offer the excuse that many of the problems are beyond his control; that the atmosphere of the company itself is the underlying factor of employee indifference. He may justify his performance by saying that it is poor human relations to crack down on employees, and besides, he can offer no incentive to employees to make a better effort. He may claim that a militant union is discouraging employee initiative, thus holding down employee productivity. And circumstances being what they are, there is little he can do about it.

He may be right in some of the things he says. Still, there is no reason for his abdication of authority. Each management assignment carries with it the responsibility for overcoming difficulties, and not for just identifying problems and explaining why they cannot be solved.

Let us talk about our individual images. Do we fear lack of acceptance by our employees? Will we be seen as less than a nice guy if we are aggressive, competitive, and tough-minded in handling conflict? Well, think of the nice-guy supervisors you know. Are they considered nice guys and also respected as managers who fulfill their responsibility in a firm and fair manner? Or are they considered nice guys, but weak managers? Some nice-guy supervisors, through lack of moral courage to face issues, have lost the respect of their employees and lost control of their jobs. Respect is something that must be earned, and without it good leadership is impossible. Some supervisors relax standards of performance for a subordinate because they are aware that personal or emotional problems of that employee make it impossible for him to do an effective job. They do so at the expense of their company and to the detriment of every other employee under their direction.

Your aggressive management methods, coupled with sound judgment, will demonstrate that you are greater than the opportunity you have. This may open the way to positions of greater responsibility in which you may exercise your full abilities.

Let us recap a little. We have stated, in so many words, that a manager must use positive leadership and have the guts to be abrasive if necessary. We have stated that our intent is not to create conflict but to be ready to meet and resolve conflict. When should this be done? Every day. You must make on-the-spot corrections every day as the need occurs. Often we spend countless hours not facing a problem, trying to find a compromise that we hope will make everyone happy. This approach is deadly on the productive pay-off per hour in your time applied to the job. Don't toss and turn repeatedly with a problem caused by an inefficient subordinate. He is the one who should be troubled by the problem, and he is the one who should be doing something about it. The issue must be faced sometime, and every day the problem can grow that much larger. Worst of all, if you accept inferior performance long enough, it becomes standard performance by default.

Okay. So competition and current conditions are bringing our business and our managers down to brass tacks. These demands are not new; they have always existed. However, they must now all be met, since we managers have been stripped of all insulation from the dangers of inefficiency. We are not disposing of our human relations techniques, for they have a proper place in management. We must, however, put employer-employee relationships on a sound give-and-take basis that is most likely to develop mature people—that is, people conscious of their responsibilities and capable of fulfilling them like intelligent adults. Employees respond quickly to firm, confident leadership. It is human nature to want to be on a winning team.

Let's consider for a moment the development of a good employer-employee relationship. Can you have positive leadership without discipline? I don't think so. A good understanding of the meaning of discipline will help us in our provision of positive leadership. Let us take a more in-depth look at this subject of discipline.

In your job as supervisor, discipline is a practical, day-to-day reality. It is up to you to maintain it by establishing a working climate in which employees want to respond to discipline. With few exceptions, people prefer to be part of a well-trained, productive working unit rather than one in which leadership is lax, rules are disregarded, and standards are so low that there is no incentive to achieve.

Employees like the challenge of constructive discipline and they respect the leader who applies it. They want to know what is expected of them. Their jobs give them greater satisfaction when their work accomplishes something. Employees do not object to reasonable orders. They have a greater sense of direction when they are governed by practical regulations that they understand are in their own self-interest and that promote the welfare of the whole organization. What they want is positive leadership. When they get it, there is seldom a problem of discipline—the group enforces its own. Discipline, then, is the product of leadership.

A supervisor's troubles in manpower management never come from discipline itself; they come from the absence of it. Discipline, taken in its narrow meaning of punishment, is the corrective action a supervisor takes to restore order to the group when one of its members violates the rules.

Even then, the supervisor who exercises leadership seldom imposes a penalty on an employee for an infraction of discipline until he has pointed out his shortcomings, discussed them with him, warned him of their consequences and done his best to persuade the employee to conform voluntarily to sound disciplinary standards. He does this because he knows that the key to discipline is self-interest and, when an employee is persuaded by words or by example that self-discipline is in his own best interest, he will look upon the supervisor as a leader, not a policeman. Over the long haul, sound discipline can never be achieved successfully by a rigid code of "don't" regulations, with a fixed forfeit automatically applied each time one is breached. Any supervisor who relies solely on punitive discipline to gain his objectives is putting a tremendous burden on himself. His planning must be perfect, his instructions detailed and absolutely accurate, and in his follow-up he must breathe down the employee's neck.

He can't afford to make mistakes. He knows that his orders will be carried out literally, that his attitude cuts off communications "coming up," and that he won't know about operational snarls unless he discovers them himself. He knows that, unless he's around to keep things moving, nothing much gets done. People are afraid to take action on their own, because it might displease him.

Anyone who takes this narrow road to discipline is cutting out a Herculean job for himself—and he had better be sure his "do-it-yourself" leadership kit is packed with all he needs to do the work, because he probably won't get any help along the way.

If a discipline program is to pay off in cooperative efficiency and high morale, it must be wisely administered by a supervisor who knows how to deal with different kinds of people reacting in different ways to a variety of situations. That's why the problem of discipline is as complex as human nature itself. But the time you spend in improving your ability to develop a disciplined workforce is time invested in enlarging your skills as a manager.

When you help employees develop discipline in work habits and on-the-job behavior, you educate them in their assignments, encourage them to get the most out of their talents, train them to work together as a team, strengthen individual self-respect and self-confidence, and add to the maturity and stability of your workforce. From this, you can see that discipline is the foundation of successful management—and that without it, organization cannot exist.

To manage well, you must have controls, and "discipline" is sometimes described as the system of rules or standards that guides the conduct of an enterprise. Finally, you must have the authority to compel obedience, if that is the only way to get compliance with company rules.

But again, the objective of a discipline program is to get employee co-operation—not merely to enforce authority. The real purpose of constructive discipline is to gain employee support in accomplishing your aims, while an immediate goal is to build a spirit of mutual respect between you and your employees. Getting this cooperation, however, requires effective daily administration of a discipline program. The following checklist may be useful to you in making sure you're not missing any bets in helping employees become disciplined workers:

1. Understand your discipline responsibilities.

The skilled supervisor earns the respect of his men through his judgment, his fairness, and his knowledge of the job. His decisions are trusted because subordinates have learned from experience that being liked is not a sure road to success, but the esteem of subordinates, earned through performance, is the best means of assuring the self-discipline of his people.

2. Make sure employees receive sound instructions.

The employee who is half-taught is half-disciplined, for discipline means knowledge. That's why untrained or partially trained employees are undisciplined. They don't like it, and they may take their dislike out on a supervisor who neglects to give them the coaching they need to improve themselves and increase their opportunities for advancement.

3. Insist on high standards of performance.

The employee who does a so-so job and gets by with it has little incentive to do a better one. What's more, he is likely to be contemptuous of a boss who pays him good money and asks almost nothing in return.

4. Maintain effective communication.

The day a new employee enters your work group, start making him a part of your operations. Explain what is expected of him, and when his work doesn't measure up, tell him so—and why. Be sure he understands the rules of your department and the reasons for them. Encourage him to suggest ways to improve not only his own performance, but also operations in general. Recognize his accomplishments and give him credit for them. Quick two-way communication sparked by mutual respect and the desire of both the supervisor and employees to reach a common goal are hallmarks of constructive discipline.

5. Enforce discipline fairly.

Don't close your eyes to any lapse in discipline. A capable supervisor sees that rules apply equally to all people: he has no favorites. When there is an offense against discipline—a broken regulation, an inferior performance—he quickly takes steps to get all the discipline and bases his action on the degrees of seriousness of the offense and the record of the offender. He considers mitigating circumstances. He tries always to find the fact behind the act, because he knows that if he can discover the reason for an employee's attitude, or what caused him to break a rule, he will be better able to give constructive advice, which builds good discipline.

6. Set the pace for discipline.

Discipline begins at home—if you can't discipline yourself, you can't expect discipline from others. The disciplined supervisor has planned and organized his job. He knows what he wants done and how. There's no lost motion; no indecision. Such a supervisor realizes that effective leadership is based on consistency. The standards he asks employees to meet don't go up and down like an elevator, according to his mood. Pressure for top performance is steady, and rules are always enforced with firmness. This kind of supervisor asks much of his subordinates, and he gets it. The reason: he asks more of himself.

The messages in this presentation deserve your serious consideration; they affect your future. Stand up now and be counted as a manager. Be positive, firm, intelligent, aggressive, and competitive. Where conflict arises, meet it eyeball to eyeball! These positive leadership methods are demanded of you as a manager. Successful fulfillment of your management responsibility is not possible without positive management.